HOW TO SURVIVE
RETIREMENT

REINVENTING YOURSELF FOR THE LIFE YOU'VE ALWAYS WANTED

HOW TO SURVIVE
RETIREMENT

REINVENTING YOURSELF FOR THE LIFE YOU'VE ALWAYS WANTED

STEVEN D. PRICE

Skyhorse Publishing

Skyhorse Publishing books may be purchased in bulk at special discounts for sales promotion, corporate gifts, fund-raising, or educational purposes. Special editions can also be created to specifications. For details, contact the Special Sales Department, Skyhorse Publishing, 307 West 36th Street, 11th Floor, New York, NY 10018 or info@skyhorsepublishing.com.

Skyhorse® and Skyhorse Publishing® are registered trademarks of Skyhorse Publishing, Inc.®, a Delaware corporation.

Visit our website at www.skyhorsepublishing.com.

10 9 8 7 6 5 4 3 2 1

Library of Congress Cataloging-in-Publication Data is available on file.

Cover photo credit: Thinkstock by Getty Images

Interior photo credits: p. xviii, Thinkstock Photos; p. 9, Shutterstock Photos; p. 14, Thinkstock Photos; p. 16, Shutterstock Photos; p. 24, Thinkstock Photos; p. 29, Shutterstock Photos; p. 36, Thinkstock Photos; p. 40, Shutterstock Photos; p. 60, Thinkstock Photos; p. 68, Shutterstock Photos; p.76, Thinkstock Photos; p.78, Shutterstock Photos; p.86, Thinkstock Photos; p.90, Shutterstock Photos; p.94, Thinkstock Photos; p. 102, Shutterstock Photos

ISBN: 978-1-63220-695-4
Ebook ISBN: 978-1-63220-996-2

Printed in the United States of America

Plans are nothing; planning is everything.
—Dwight D. Eisenhower

CONTENTS

PREFACE

O, blest retirement! friend to life's decline—
How blest is he who crowns, in shades like these,
A youth of labor with an age of ease!
                                    —Oliver Goldsmith

My vagabond writing career of more than four decades must give the impression that I've played grasshopper to other people's ants. That's another way of saying that several people on the verge of retirement have now sought my counsel about what to do with the vast amounts of leisure time that loomed ahead of them. One went so far as to buy me lunch in exchange for picking my brain.

"Okay, what do you like to do?" I asked after the waiter took our orders.

"Um, I enjoy my job, but I don't want to stay in business. I'm crazy about golf, but I can't see myself playing three hundred days a year."

Fair enough. "Well, how do you spend your weekends? When you're not on the course?"

"Knocking around the apartment. Visiting with the kids and grand-kids. Watching TV—sports, Netflix . . . you know, basic stuff. But I can't see myself doing that for the rest of my life."

"How about vacations?" I asked. "Aside from the golf?"

"No golf on vacations. Not since my wife and I started spending three weeks a summer in France. A week in Paris and two in a rental cottage in a small town in Brittany. My wife likes the solitude—she has a pretty high-pressure job too. Not a golf course in sight."

A thought dawned on me. "Do you speak the language?"

"Not since high school. Everyone there understands English."

"They'll love you to death if you speak their language. The Alliance Français here in New York City has a one-on-one conversation program. You could probably find a French-speaking teacher somewhere else for in-home tutorials if you prefer."

My friend nodded. "Makes sense."

"Do you cook?" I asked.

"Oh, pancakes for the grandkids."

"Make that crêpes—take a cooking course."

Fade out the lunch, fade in a year later: the guy took my advice and can now *parlez-vous* up a storm with the natives.

When others approached me with similar questions, at first I found it hard to believe that they had no interests that would spill over into retirement years. My reaction revealed a generous helping of egocentricity: many interests fill my hours when I'm not working, and—full grasshopper disclosure here—sometimes when I should be working. However, like the fellow who couldn't see himself playing golf every day, not everyone has hobbies, sports, and other interests that would both continue into and consume one's golden years.

That leaves reinvention, one of retirement counselors' favorite buzzwords and essential to avoid languishing with boredom or worse.

* * * * * *

Widespread retirement is a relatively new phenomenon. Before the end of World War II, only those who had earned, inherited, or married wealthy could afford to stop working when they reached the end of their careers. Our less distinguished ancestors were obliged to toil until they died in harness, so to speak. If and when the inevitable illness or injury forced them to stop, their families looked after them or else they became objects of charity however they could find it.

The twentieth century brought a radical change. The Social Security Act of 1935 and post–World War II prosperity provided the ways and means for older people to consider retirement. In its beginning, Social Security kicked in for anyone age sixty-five at a time when life expectancy was sixty for men and three years more for women. If your parents, grandparents, or great-grandparents made it past sixty-five, although they were living on actuarially borrowed time, they were still alive. And they were likely to afford to enjoy their leisure years because the upward-spiraling cost of living didn't erode Social Security and pension checks the way it now does.

Thanks to advances in medicine, nutrition, and technology, American life expectancy started to rise, and it continues to do so: 77.4 years for men and 82.2 years for women of 2013. That means retirees now have more time to fill, either at work or in retirement. And in retirement, reinvention—there's that phrase again—becomes even more important.

* * * * * *

All who retire discover that Time (with a capital T) can be both friend and foe. Your week as well as your life revolved around the job for many decades. Assuming that you put in an eight-hour day and managed to sleep for eight hours, you had eight more to yourself. If you commuted some distance from your workplace, your free time might have dropped to six hours. Factor in household chores and other family responsibilities, and you might have had three hours to your own self. Not too bad—plenty of time to catch a movie or watch TV or read a book or go for an early-morning or late-afternoon jog.

With retirement, however, comes a great chunk of free time. Just do the math:

You now have 112 hours a week (168 hours in a week minus 8 hours of sleep × 7 days) instead of the 88 (168 to 140 of work and 40 of sleep) when you worked. And don't forget that you now have no more commuting time or business trips. If you have no health or family hindrances, you have before you "a month of Sundays."

Those extra twenty-four hours a week—think of it as two extra full days—can be a blessing or a curse. It all depends on how you fill your time, and that's one of the reasons for this book. We'll explore such areas as the following:

- **Recreation:** Did you always have a hankering to play the piano but never thought you had time to practice? Or did you play the guitar as a kid and regretted giving it up? Have you dreamed about fishing trips, but something always got in the way? How about those needlepoint projects that you started a dozen years ago and that have been gathering dust in the attic ever since? Retirement gives you the time literally to recreate yourself through a sport, game, or hobby that you always wanted to try or that you haven't done in years.

- **Education:** Like the now-French-speaking retiree, you now have the time to explore avenues that lead to expanding intellectual and cultural horizons. Learn a language or a musical instrument or go back to one you once studied. Take a course in a subject that grabs you. Travel throughout the country and the world by yourself, with a companion, or in a group sponsored by special- or general-interest tour organizations.

- **Volunteering:** You may not realize the depth and breadth of talents and enthusiasms that you have acquired over the years. They're waiting to be used in the service of others. Your town, city, or county contains dozens of organizations that will welcome the time and energies you have to offer. And, when you do, you'll discover the satisfaction that volunteerism gives.

- **Relocating:** The horrific winter of 2014 caused any number of sufferers, regardless of age, to dream about warmer climates. "You know," said one New England resident as he dug his car out of a snowdrift, "I used to joke about the old folks who moved to Florida. Now that I'm no longer a kid, I stand in awe of how sensible they were."

Moving to an area with better weather is only one reason for a retiree to relocate. Many older people come to realize that suburbs and the country were fine when driving wasn't an issue. However, when driving becomes a problem, they look to cities that have public transportation. In addition, urban medical, cultural, and recreational facilities are more convenient to get to, while food, medications, and just about everything else can be delivered.

Other reasons to relocate include living in apartments and houses that are now too large or too expensive to maintain or present physical challenges to older residents that can't be made more accommodating. Neighborhoods and other areas change, and not always for the better. Consider moving closer to children and grandchildren who live in a different part of the state or country. Retirement and assisted-living facilities and communities offer social, physical, and medical advantages.

We'll help you consider whether relocating makes sense and, if so, how to go about it.

- **Vacations:** Once upon a time we might have hitchhiked and backpacked around the country or abroad or piled into a car and headed for a week at a beach. Now that the constraints of age and maturity (not always synonymous) have caught up with us, our holidaying wants and needs have changed. Intergenerational vacations with children and grandchildren may be the answer, as might tours and cruises that cater to seniors.
- **Finances:** Retirement magazines and TV commercials depict happy and healthy seniors enjoying their golden years with nary a worry in the world. Although we all pray that such a picture will be the template for our lives, such is not always the case. Although you may have thought that you and your advisors had created an adequate financial blueprint, circumstances change. Some changes, such as moving to a new residence, will be of your own making. Others, like unforeseen medical

expenses and investment portfolio upheavals, are beyond your control. Whatever the cause, you'll need to know how to handle your assets in the light of new conditions.

However, the specifics of one's financial situation differ from person to person; one size does not fit all. That's why this book won't go into specific strategies applicable to your particular situation, whatever it might be; it's up to you and your accountant or wealth manager to determine what's best for you.

- **Going Back To Work:** Returning to the workforce wouldn't be of your own choosing if your financial circumstances changed for the worse and you needed the income. However, even if you're well situated, your inner entrepreneurial spirit can prove overwhelming or indeed emerge at this later stage of life. Many retirees have started their own business in new fields or have signed on to an existing enterprise for fun and profit. Whether the reason is voluntary or involuntary, you'll have to know how to find what's available and how successfully to embark on a second career.
- **Health:** The change of lifestyle that retirement brings can have a severe impact on your health. A classic example is someone whose occupation involved physical activity and who is now sedentary. Finding ways to stay in shape physically, mentally, and emotionally is a key to enjoying retirement to the fullest. Getting up off the couch, turning off the TV, and putting away the potato chips is the first step to a beneficial and—yes—enjoyable regimen of diet and exercise.

Then, too, the aging process brings changes to our bodies and minds. Coming to terms with that unavoidable fact of life is important, and so is learning to recognize which changes are or aren't normal and natural. Thanks to a doctor friend, this book has a lengthy chapter on the very subject.

* * * * * *

The word *retirement* can mean "withdrawn" and "end of usefulness."
But it needn't and shouldn't. Read on, and learn how to make a new
place in the real world for yourself and your loved ones by enlarging
and enhancing your own universe.

Steven D. Price

ACKNOWLEDGMENTS

With gratitude to the many people who shared their personal and professional views and experiences, most notably:

Tony Ard, Hank Beebe, Chris Carpenter, Mike Cohen, Norman Fine, Arnie Fleischer, John Friedland, Rich Goldman, Neal Goldman, Jack Hagele, Matthew Lagoy, Nick Lyons, Arthur Liblit, Dr. Irwin Light, Dr. Ruth Mechaneck, Stan Meierfeld, Elliot Merberg, Beth Rowland, Fred Sagarin, Jenene Stookesberry, Myron Weiss, and Betsy Wesman.

And to Carmelo "Candy" Candito, the indomitable nonagenarian who does weekly volunteer work by distributing flowers sent to patients at the Memorial Sloan Kettering Hospital.

Special thanks to Laurence Burd, MD, for the chapter on health issues, and to my editor Niels Aaboe.

1

ENTERING RETIREMENT

"Retirement may be looked upon either as a prolonged holiday or as a rejection, a being thrown on to the scrap-heap."
—Simone de Beauvoir

Madame de Beauvoir's observation is an excellent, if grim, way to approach the subject of retirement. Some people facing departure from the workforce do so with a sigh of relief and a deep smile of satisfaction. They're the ones who planned ahead to make sure they have an adequate financial cushion or, although less likely, who come upon a windfall in the form of selling one's business for big bucks, hitting the lottery for a dream payoff (hey, it can happen), or coming into money through marriage or inheritance. They accept the fact that they paid their dues on the job, but time marches on and it's time to call it quits. They know how, where, and with whom they want to spend their declining years—yes, "declining," because they also face the inevitable fact that "the old gray mare, she ain't what she/he used to be," and, like the aged equines, they will continue to grow long in the tooth.

Yes, blessed are they who retire with such an attitude and with sufficient resources to make a seamless transition to another stage of life. However, fewer and fewer of us will have such a cloudless blue sky. Therefore, much of how you'll feel about facing the future will depend on the circumstances that surround your leave-taking.

* * * * * *

Easy transitions into retirement are becoming rarer and rarer. The days when a valued employee toiled until age sixty-five, received a gold watch and a hearty handclasp from the boss at a retirement dinner, and then spent the remaining "golden years" puttering in a garden, collecting stamps, or playing checkers at the lodge hall are receding into the mists of time. On the other hand, retirements have become as much forced as they are voluntary. Companies downsize or outsource individual jobs and entire departments and divisions. They relocate or go bankrupt. They implement new technologies that require different and usually more complex skill sets. Employees at all levels who fully expected to work for another decade or more find themselves adrift and unable to contend with the present job market.

The last example above hit home to members of the domestic-travel and meeting-planning department at a large, multinational corporation. The department was outsourcing to another country, leaving some thirty employees without jobs. Several were in their mid- to late sixties and planned to retire within the next few years, so the announcement that the department was being eliminated, while startling, didn't dismay them. Younger ones, especially administrative assistants, were able to find positions in other departments. If they didn't, they believed with youthful self-assurance that they would land on their feet in record time.

The unhappiest employees, with good reason, were the fifty-somethings. Many were no longer full of energy, drive, and optimism, and they were well aware of the tight job market, especially for workers in their age bracket. Severance pay might tide them over for a while, but unemployment insurance alone would not sustain them, nor would eroded 401(k) revenues, revenues that are subject to penalties for early withdrawal. Although some had working spouses, others didn't. Many had children to support, including the grown children who couldn't find a job and were living at home. To say they were traumatized would be understatement.

"I felt as though the moon and stars hit me," one later recalled. "My initial reaction was 'I'm all washed up.' Although my supervisor kept reassuring me that my being handed my walking papers had absolutely nothing to do with my job performance or my personality, I couldn't help personalize the situation. 'Nothing to do with me? The hell it doesn't—it's only my life!' That's also what I told the poor human resources administrator who had the bad luck to be the one who gave me my exit interview. She had to ask me form questions like 'Did you enjoy your job? Have you any recommendations about your position that might improve the company?' I'm sorry to admit I hit the ceiling—'yes, I enjoyed my job,' I told her, 'now give it back to me,' although I used stronger language than that.

"The one positive thing that the HR administrator did when I had finished my rant was to suggest I see a retirement coach, someone who could help ease the emotional aspects of the transition. In spite of my agitated state, I was able to see the value of such help, and I took the coach's contact information. When I felt in a more receptive frame of mind, I had a few sessions. Talking things through helped a lot. In fact, I'm now considering going into that line of work. Hell, I have the experience for it."

Being forced to leave a professional partnership—whether a law firm, group medical practice, architecture firm, or another variety—is fraught with emotional consequences. You may have once been your law firm's "rainmaker," bringing in new business right and left, but your connections in the business world and in certain industries grew progressively weaker with the passage of time. And just as your connections were fading, a younger lawyer whom your firm had been courting because of her rainmaking abilities decided to join. Shortly thereafter came the news that your services were no longer needed.

Or a "boutique" specialty department of another law firm has seen the handwriting on the wall that the firm was in serious financial trouble. For that firm, getting out while the getting was good made sense, and the lawyers moved en masse to your firm. Unfortunately for you, their specialty was yours, and the new team convinced your firm's partners that they could get along quite nicely without you. In these uneasy economic times, the firm's executive committee agreed.

In either instance, even with a substantial buyout package, you found yourself with your tail between your legs when you left the offices where you spent the past forty-five years. Your feelings were injured, and you had a sense of dread that your productive life was as dead as the firm's founders whose portraits hung on the reception area walls.

That was the experience of a lawyer who stayed on at his firm with the designation of "counsel" when he retired. Although no longer a partner, he went into the office or stayed in touch in case he was needed for consultation work. Much to his dismay and chagrin, his opinion was rarely sought, much as he prowled the corridors offering assistance. Nor were fellow lawyers terribly eager to include him in lunches or other social plans above and beyond office parties. Tired of swallowing bitter pills, he bowed out as gracefully as possible until, like *Alice in Wonderland*'s Cheshire Cat, he gradually disappeared and only his name remained on the firm's letterhead.

Equally, if not even more, emotionally difficult is a forced retirement from a family business. The classic example of siblings ganging up on one of their own for a variety of reasons often has nothing to do with the retiree's job performance. Somewhat less prevalent is the case of children who decide that a parent who built the business up from nothing no longer has the "vision" or "energy" to continue at the helm.

One such example of the latter involved a small, family-owned hardware chain. Grandpa opened the first store when the community was a small town. He expanded the business and opened two other stores as the town became a city with expanding suburbs. When his two sons joined the business, they became restless and thought about new worlds to conquer. The nursery business appealed to them, since their stores already carried many of the necessary gardening tools.

Dad took an instant dislike to the idea. He and his sons hadn't a clue about running a garden shop, plus there were two very successful nurseries shops within a half-hour drive of all three of their stores.

The sons persisted. They accused their father of lacking the "fire in the belly" zeal that turned the one-store business into a chain (even if the chain had only three stores). When they asked their mother's opinion, Mom's siding with her boys upset her husband even further. Dad, who knew when he was beaten, quit in a fit of pique before the family-owned corporation could vote him out. "I threw in the towel," he insisted, "but they made me do it."

Another kind of involuntary retirement comes from health considerations. Catastrophic illness or accidents can strike anyone and at any age. One day you're bouncing along with a spring in your step and the world on a string, and the next day you're in a medical office or a hospital bed facing a doctor with a grim look on his face and a grimmer message on his lips. Or, if the bad news doesn't apply to you, it well may happen to a loved one.

Or a sudden event can be life-altering. A butcher in his late fifties was momentarily distracted while hacking a rack of lamb into individual chops. The result was the loss of four fingers. A commercial airline pilot had a bad spill on the ski slopes that affected his eyesight and prevented him from flying again.

Those who become disabled are likely to have serious financial as well as medical concerns, and the rest of their lives will become circumscribed by physical or emotional boundaries. The extent of the limitations will determine the extent to which you can reinvent your retirement. When a parent, spouse, child, or another close loved one is the patient, you may have to make the tough decision to leave your job and become the primary caregiver. That too will circumscribe your new life. However, as grim as the prospect may first appear, rest assured that there are ways, as subsequent chapters of this book will show, that you can make the most of the free time you carve out of your schedule. And yes, you must find time to and for yourself. If not, you'll wear yourself down until you're a physical and emotional wreck who's of little to no use to the person for whom you're caring.

* * * * * *

As we've seen, retirement's early stages involve changes of attitude toward all manner of things. Departure requires a letting go, and among your initial tasks is to determine and then to accept what you must relinquish. In other words, retirement is a process, not an event, and, like other transitions, there are psychological rewards and pitfalls.

The work world is to a large extent predictable and dependable, structured according to job requirements. Success is based on performance. If you haven't left your job to become a caregiver, you're now in a realm that's the complete opposite. Life now is a *tabula rasa,* a blank slate to be filled in however you wish. Accomplishment now depends not on monetary rewards, but on finding satisfaction in whatever fruitful and fulfilling life you create for yourself.

Being single both simplifies and complicates retirement. You have only yourself to look after. You can make your own choices. On the other hand, you don't have a partner to share things with or lean on emotionally or financially. Most people have a need to nurture and be nurtured. Being a single retiree may lead to isolation and loneliness, which can be the first step to abusing alcohol or other "self-medicating" substances.*

---

* Alcoholism among seniors is a far more serious problem than most of us realize. Conservative estimates indicate that problem drinking affects some 17 percent of all adults above the age of sixty. That figure may be an underestimation because relatives, friends, and physicians often attribute physical and emotional indications of alcohol abuse to similar symptoms of age-related conditions.

* * * * * *

In light of the above, let's take a moment to examine your attitude toward the position you're about to leave. Your job involved, to a greater or lesser extent, authority and responsibilities. Both are facets of power and attention, and you don't have to be Gordon Gekko, Jay Gatsby, or King Lear to understand or crave the attraction. You basked in the influence you wielded among subordinates who sought your wisdom that came from workplace and life experience. And you were flattered and felt a sense of accomplishment when superiors, equals, and underlings praised your accomplishments, whether by a kind word and a pat on the back, a glowing mention in the company newsletter, or a salary increase or bonus.

Them days will be gone forever, my friend. Retirement necessarily means a loss of influence, authority, attention, and admiration (or, if you're that kind of person, being feared). If you're middle management, there's no more telling subordinates what to do and holding them responsible when they make mistakes. No more assessing their jobs and bestowing or withholding salary increases. If you're upper-upper management, you'll lose the use of a company car or a seat on the corporate jet, all-expense-paid meetings in exotic and glamorous destinations, and the opportunity to be on a first-name basis with industry movers-and-shakers. Some executives liked the feeling of being fawned over by headwaiters and concierges during expense-account lunches and business trips. Postretirement, they become just plain Joe or Jane, and that can be a traumatic shock.

Unless you're independently wealthy, have the investment acumen of a Warren Buffett, leave your company with a golden parachute, or are far better at saving money than the rest of us are, retirement leads to a drop in financial resources. That holds true even with Social Security, pension payments, and other sources of income. If you don't think that will be the case, just wait till you see your bank statement and credit or debit card bill at the end of the month.

Once upon a time you could charge business lunches as expenses to the company. Now the cost comes out of your pocket if you're joining former business associates for an expensive lunch or going on a trip that used to be paid for by your ex-employer under the heading of "goodwill."

Salesmen, teachers, clergymen, professional athletes, and other "people persons" who are accustomed to being surrounded by and interacting with others on a daily basis will find themselves isolated to varying degrees. At first you may give a sigh of relief and tell family and friends, "Thank heavens I'm out of the rat race." Then, however, the lack of people around you may gnaw at you. Salespeople, for example, who for decades have been out in the marketplace with a smile and a shine and a ready quip, now wonder "Where'd everybody go?"

In an effort to socialize, you'll phone former business associates to catch up on office gossip, but they have work to do and less time to schmooze than you wish they had. You meet them for lunch, prepared to spend the better part of the afternoon, but they glance at their watches or cell phones and start to fidget after the second cup of coffee. You meet again in six months, but by then the players in office politics will have changed, and you find yourself nodding knowingly without having a clue about whom or what your companion is describing. You may also learn that the hotshot youngster who now has your position has changed all the systems you had carefully created and implemented, and, although the person sitting across the table is trying to be polite, you can see he or she couldn't care less about your granddaughter's sophomore college year.

* * * * * *

Distinguishing between the emotional and the physical consequences of retirement is difficult because the two are so often inextricably joined. Hints or solid evidence of the physical changes that come with age— receding hairline, receding gums, weight gain, and diminished sex drive and/or performance, among others—point inexorably toward old age

and beyond. Add the decline with a postretirement loss of authority or self-worth, and you have the ingredients for depression.

We all know people who do their best (or worst) to stave off being carried away by Time's winged chariot. Men try to retain or recapture their younger macho days by dressing and acting younger, swaggering in front of younger women, and being "one of the guys" with their young sons or grandsons. Women become "flirty," invest in cosmetic surgery nips and tucks to recapture their drop-dead-gorgeous days, and adopt their daughters' or granddaughters' fashions and slang. Although such age-inappropriate behavior, which is what advice columnists call it, may make you feel better over the short haul, it wears off, and you're back to what you see in the mirror and what you hear and see yourself saying and doing.

* * * * * *

Grandparents who enter retirement and who live near their children often find themselves faced with the "Mom/Dad, do me a favor . . ."

syndrome. Your son or daughter may phone or text to ask you to pick up little Heather after soccer practice or take Jeff to the dentist or to ask that you babysit for an afternoon or evening. All well and good if you have the time and inclination, but there will be occasions when you must explain that you have something else to do and, no, you can't or won't reshuffle your schedule unless an emergency occurs. Making yourself available at every beck and call will lead to resentment that can be avoided by asserting your right to decide how you will spend your days and nights.

* * * * * *

Couples who are married and retire together often are faced with a new set of challenges. Now, rather than having time to get out and socialize at work or having time to themselves, they are around each other more often. Performing simple duties around the house, deciding who plans finances, or spending time together can become difficult if two retirees do not share common interests. Frequent time together and lack of privacy can also cause a strain in the marriage and ultimately lead to bickering or even more hostile relations. As the old line goes, "I married him/her for better or worse, not for lunch."

Another source of tension may come when one spouse retires before the other can or chooses to. A retiring spouse who enjoys some of the homier chores like grocery shopping and cooking makes a positive contribution to the relationship. On the other hand, when the retiree spends the day waiting for the partner, who's tired after a long day of work, to come home to do chores or to go out and socialize with friends, the result is resentment on both sides. The working partner may not be sympathetic to the retiree's desire for activity, while the retiree may be uneasy or indeed envious that the worker still has a life very much outside the home. The best result is achieved when the retiree finds a fulfilling new set of activities with "How was your day?" conversations to share.

These dilemmas are a strong argument for couples deciding prior to retirement what they'd like to do with their lives. Remember when you two were dating seriously enough to contemplate spending your lives together? That was the point where "What do you want out of life?" questions crept into conversations, with the answers being important factors in that "call the caterer" decision. Well, that was then and this is now, but the questions need to be asked again, this time with retirement in mind even though only one of you is contemplating leaving or being forced to leave a job. Where might you want to live? What will you like to do with your leisure time—apart and together? Who'll do the chores? How shall we handle the finances? How well are we prepared for inevitable medical issues? Even if you can't answer these questions now with any degree of certainty, you must take the time and effort to raise the questions. And *effort* is the right word because some compromise is likely to be involved; if you two haven't learned how to agree to disagree, now's the time, folks.

* * * * * *

Physicians and social scientists have observed that being subjected to enforced retirement can be the equivalent of mourning the death of a loved one. Elisabeth Kübler-Ross, a pioneer psychiatrist in counseling patients who were devastated by an actual or impending loss, summarized five steps in the grieving process. (Not all five steps are always experienced or, if they are, not necessarily in the order that Dr. Kübler-Ross proposed.)

The first stage is denial. Even with a pink slip in the pay envelope or a security guard helping you pack your personal effects, you don't believe it's happening to you. You've been at your job for decades, you've always done your work to everyone's satisfaction and then some, and your supervisor's spouse is your spouse's second cousin. No, you say with certainty, there must be some mistake.

The second stage is anger. You accept that you've been let go, and you're mad as hell. Your former boss and his people are a bunch of ingrates who deserve everything bad that will happen to the company. You look forward to the day the company's stock tanks, its products are recalled, government investigators throw the book at the crooks who run the show . . . you'll dance on their graves. (The same feeling of anger can be directed at the patient for whom you "voluntarily" retired to become a caregiver. You're unhappy, so you take it out on the hapless patient as if the medical condition were his or her fault.)

The third step involves bargaining, based on the classic grieving stage of "I promise to be a better person if only my late spouse would come back." You imagine strategies that you can use to regain your job. You'll admit to errors you think you made in the past (even if most are figments of your imagination), move to a new department, and/or forgo salary raises and bonuses if only you're given another chance.

The fourth stage is depression, which can be the most devastating. It bears repeating that depression can force you into mental and physical inactivity, sapping your energies when you most need them. A wonderful metaphor for such desperate isolation occurs in a scene in the movie *The Graduate,* in which Benjamin is drifting in his scuba suit in the family swimming pool, floating but emotionally sinking. Like him, you lose interest in things you once enjoyed and spend all your time brooding (sorry, but you can't count on a Mrs. Robinson or the male equivalent). You eat and drink too much, and usually the wrong things. You snap at loved ones who offer love and support ("Don't pity me!—I can't stand being pitied!"). The only emotions you feel are jealousy and anger at anyone having a good time.

And you wallow in self-pity. You believe you have no value: if you couldn't hold on to your job, how can you be expected to find another one? You sometimes take yourself to task for ruining your life by a slavelike devotion to your occupation. You find yourself regretting what you forfeited en route to business success. You lost chances for greater closeness with your spouse and an appreciation of what he or she went through to help you advance. You distanced yourself from children and grandchildren whom you hurt by missing a school play or softball championship game. You alienated old, formerly dear friends for whom you didn't have time. You never allowed yourself time to develop interests and enthusiasms that would have made you a well-rounded and joyful person. And for what?

Because this depressed stage becomes very destructive if and when it lasts too long, professional help in the form of counseling is not only appropriate but also essential. "Too long" is a relative term, and it's up to family and friends to speak up or, if necessary, take stronger intervention steps when they feel that professional help is the only thing that stands between the retiree and the likelihood of permanent emotional or physical damage.

Blessed relief comes at the fifth stage, which is that of acceptance. Whether on your own or with professional assistance, you come out of your indecisiveness, floundering, lethargy, or deep depression and acknowledge your new situation. You're no longer consumed by rage or despair. You have your energy back, and you're ready—even eager—to go on with the rest of your life, whatever that may hold.

* * * * * *

That's the upbeat, optimistic attitude that the balance of this book embraces. A psychiatrist who has observed many pre- and postretirement relatives, friends, and acquaintances and who has treated many others as patients summed up the option very succinctly: retirement brings with it the opportunity to expand or contract one's life.

Now let's find ways to expand it.

2

DISCOVERING THE NEW YOU

"Once you're over the hill, you begin to pick up speed."
—Charles M. Schulz

Many people who have taken voluntary retirement liken their reaction to the first day of grade-school summer vacation, and even some of those who have been fired have the same feeling of "No more pencils, no more books!" glee. Others liken the first few weeks or months as a sort of honeymoon—the joy of getting to know a new and much-anticipated partner called "leisure."

Some fledgling retirees spend their "honeymoon" doing nothing, just simply basking in sweet nothingness that Italians call *dolce far niente*. They stay up late at night and watch TV, DVDs, or web-streamed entertainment and then sleep till all hours of the morning. They take long lunches followed by siestas. They go to movie matinees, when theaters have no long lines or fidgety kids or texting teenagers who are sitting in the row in front of them. They play in afternoon pinochle or cribbage games at the lodge hall or play bridge with "the girls." They take midweek fishing trips where they and equally footloose pals have the stream or lake to themselves. Or they stay home and have cocktails and dinner at their own pace. That is to say, they savor the joyous, unbridled freedom of "a month of Sundays."

However, there comes a point—weeks, months, or longer—when most retirees realize that there must be more to life than what they've been doing. Although they had looked forward to their newfound freedom, they felt that they weren't making the most of that freedom. There has to be more to life. The question is, What's next? What's the secret to charting a happy and fulfilling course for the rest of your life?

* * * * * *

The first step is to decide what will make you happy and fulfilled. Several retirement experts suggest sitting down with pencil and paper or tablet or in front of a computer and making a list that will help you focus on and define your retirement goals. Don't think of the exercise as a test. No one, especially yourself, should be grading or judging you. Instead, this exercise is a way to create a profile that will shed light on aspects of your past and present life. The goal is to discover highways and byways that lead toward the "new you."

Although the following questions are phrased in the present tense, answer them as if they were in the past tense as well. For example, as you consider whether you enjoy a particular sport now, include your childhood, adolescence, and young adulthood. In this regard, many people have found that looking through family photo albums and scrapbooks are useful catalysts to jog memories.

Okay, here we go:

- **Physical:** Which kind of sports do you prefer—competitive or noncompetitive? That is, do you agree with legendary football coach Vince Lombardi when he said, "Winning isn't everything, it's the only thing"? Or is simply participating your greatest satisfaction? That's an important consideration for "alpha" athletes as the aging process catches up with them: tennis players will find at some point that they can't get to the ball or make the returns they made a decade earlier. Some will pronounce themselves "all washed up" and quit the sport. Others will be content with just getting out on the court, and if they lose a point because of an unforced error . . . well, that's all part of the game.

  Is tennis your game? Golf? Bicycle riding? Working out in the gym? Mall-walking? Square dancing? Or do you prefer less strenuous pursuits like yoga, gardening, croquet, or strolling around the neighborhood?

  How about the Great Outdoors: camping, canoeing/kayaking, hiking, fishing, hunting, chopping logs (remember how President Reagan loved to attack a woodpile), trail riding on horseback?

  Or none of the above? You might be the type who, as the line goes, whenever you feel like exercising, you lie down on the couch until the urge passes (not the healthiest of attitudes, of course, so consider changing your ways).

- **Mental/Intellectual:** Do you read books and magazines (in print or online form)? Serious "highbrow" stuff or "escapist" fare? Or are you not a "reader," preferring to get your news and entertainment via television, radio, and/or the Internet? Do you enjoy the challenge of crossword puzzles and other word games? How about such strategy games as chess or bridge? Do you like to discuss current events or books or articles you've read with other people, or is that a waste of time and energy?

  Think back to your student days from grade school through the highest level that you achieved. Did you like school? If so, which were your favorite subjects, and why? Which didn't you like, and why? What do you remember best about any favorite teachers? Or did academic memories leave such a sour taste in your mouth that you'd never want to take another course in anything as long as you live?

- **Hobbies:** What did you do with your leisure time when you were younger? Since you came of age in the pre-video-games era, did you like to play with model trains, or a chemistry set, or a toy kitchen? Did you enjoy board games? Performing magic and card tricks? How about collecting: stamps, coins, dolls and dollhouses, comic books, trading cards, movie and sports memorabilia, fossils, or rocks and minerals? Did you find ways to work with your hands, such as making bird-houses and other woodworking projects or doing arts and crafts like making jewelry, painting, sculpting, modeling clay, or leatherwork?

  And as you grew up, did you take up needlework: knitting, embroidery, crocheting, or needlepoint? Amateur radio or another science project? Tinkering with model or real cars?

- **Organizations:** Were you a joiner? A Cub Scout and then a Boy Scout and perhaps an Explorer or Sea Scout, or a

Brownie and then a Girl Scout? Were you drawn to a teenage civic or political or religious organization? If so, were you a leader or a follower?

Did you do volunteer work, such as working as a Candy Striper aide at a local hospital, or help out in a soup kitchen, or deliver Thanksgiving and Christmas baskets to needy families?

- **Music:** Did you play an instrument? Did you play for your own amusement or in a group? How about singing? Or was being told that you have a "tin ear" or were "tone deaf" stifle any interest in playing or singing that you might have had (and may still)? Perhaps you've always been a listener? Which type or types of music do you enjoy most? Or dislike most? Did you go to concerts? Which do you recall as outstanding?

  How about dancing? Ballroom, ballet, social, square, or clog? Or have you been told you have "two left feet" and firmly believe it to be true even though you always harbored the idea of making like Fred Astaire or Ginger Rogers, Gene Kelly or Cyd Charisse?

- **Travel:** Which were your favorite vacation destinations? Your least favorite? Are you eager to explore new locales, or are you happier returning to old familiar haunts? Did you ever spend time somewhere and think, "I wouldn't mind staying here longer or even living here?" Or are you happy to get back because there's no place like home?

* * * * * *

Delving deeper into your personal history and personality is a much trickier proposition because no one likes to consider, much less admit to, having faults or failings. If, like most of us, you have difficulty assessing yourself, ask a friend or relative for help; critical objectivity never hurts. Select someone who both knows you well and has your very best interests at heart. And if you sense your helper is being too uncomfortably judgmental for your taste, find someone else.

Periodic reviews made by your business or military superiors are another source of information. Even though it's unlikely that you saved the paperwork, you should be able to remember what you were told about your strong and weak points (unless you blocked them out).

Some of the following questions may duplicate responses that you gave in the preceding section, but they bear repeating, because coming up with a different or a finer-tuned response on sober second through is a real possibility.

- Which were/are the happiest times of your life, and why? Grade school, junior high, high school? Summer camp? College? Grad school? The military? The present? Any other period?
- Which aspects of the jobs you've had did you most like, and why? Which aspects did you most dislike, and why? And what, if anything, did you do to improve your situation?
- Are you a "people person," or do you prefer solitary activities?
- How do you feel about volunteer work? Would you seek something where you would donate your time and skills, or do you feel you should be paid for your time and energy?
- Do you often spend time thinking back on your life, or are you the type who always looks ahead? Do you regret things that happened, and do you beat yourself up over them? Or do you shrug them off as "no sense crying over spilled milk" or "water under the bridge"? Have you re-peated critical mistakes, or did you learn from them and act accordingly?
- Are you guided by emotions more than by logic, or the other way round?

- Which important decisions in your life could have been easily changed, or did you stick to your guns once you made up your mind?
- Do you stand up for your beliefs even when others hold differing views, or do you keep silent rather than risk creating friction?
- Are you reluctant to accept directions and instructions, or do you resent being told what to do—and always have?
- Similarly, do you prefer detailed, structured, and regimented activities, or are you the freewheeling "I'll wing it" type?

* * * * * *

When you've finished responding to all the questions, take a few steps back or put the list away for few hours so that you can look over your answers with a cold, clear eye. Did anything surprise you? For example . . .

- On sober reflection, are you not quite the people person you thought you were, to the extent that you suspect you'd enjoy more solitude now that you're out of the rat race?
- Do you look back with nostalgia at the model train layout you and your father built in the basement, the one you hadn't thought about in years? And would you like to find others who share that interest, such as members of a model-railroading club?
- Did you come upon a photograph of you and the family cocker spaniel while you were leafing through albums, and do you now wish you could have a dog, but your Significant Other doesn't like them?
- Was one of life's fondest memories the spontaneous getaway weekend to San Francisco that you and your husband took before your oldest child was born, and do

you wonder whether that charming restaurant in Sausalito is still there?

- Was one of the memorable parts of your job the annual outing in which you and other volunteers from the office helped escort special-needs children to the circus?

Got the picture? The purpose of these exercises is to ask yourself leading questions, the answers to which will (1) give you a better idea of who you are at this moment and (2) suggest ways to reinvent yourself into the "new you."

You've changed over the years, and just because you've reached a certain age and stage doesn't mean you can't continue to do so. Call it "growth or "reinvention," but whatever the word, you can and will grow by taking the steps and suggestions found in this book's upcoming chapters.

* * * * * *

Retirement and Financial Coaches

The questions that you've just pondered are the kind that you would be asked by a retirement coach. In this age of gurus, advisors, and other varieties of professional advice givers, add "retirement coaches" to the list. As the name suggests, they work with soon-to-be or already retired clients in the emotional, vocational, and avocational areas much the way investment counselors do with regard to finances. And some are in fact also financial planners or work closely with colleagues who are.

A wide range of people seek the help of coaches, according to Roberta Taylor, psychotherapist and board-certified coach who practices in the Boston area. "They say, 'I'm retiring next year, and I don't have a clue what I'm going to do,'" she said. "Others who are already retired and thought it would be wonderful to have free time realize, usually in a very short time, that it's not enough and they feel disconnected from people."

Many different kinds of services are available to help navigate retirement. These professionals go under the titles of retirement coaches, elder life advisers, and certified senior advisers. Services vary. A retirement coach generally will help a client develop goals and strategies, while a certified senior adviser or elder life adviser is likely to offer help with social issues, such as senior housing and health care. Be aware, however, that there is some overlap. For more information, contact the International Coach Federation (coachfederation.org) or the Society of Certified Senior Advisors (society-csa.com).

3

THE NEW REALITIES OF MONEY

"The question isn't at what age I want to retire, it's at what income."

—George Foreman

Before we travel much further along the path to reinvention, let's make sure your luggage contains an essential element. Which is to say, money.

How much money will you need over your retirement years? Comedian Henny Youngman's classic wisecrack was "I've got all the money I'll ever need if I die by four o'clock today." However, for those among us who choose to take a somewhat longer view, the answer becomes "it depends." Among relevant factors are your present age and your life expectancy (many people outlive actuarial tables, but most don't, which is why the statistics are based in reality).*

Other considerations are how many mouths you'll have to feed and for how long, your own health and that of your family members

---

* The government's Social Security life expectancy calculator is a useful tool: www.ssa.gov/planners/lifeexpectancy.htm.

who depend on you, where you live, how you live (that is, your life-style), and your present and future assets. As you can see, financial planning is by no means a "one size fits all" situation.

The first step is to create a portrait of your financial landscape, starting with assets. Determine (where applicable) and then add up income from, in no particular order, your 401(k) pension, IRAs, other investments, Social Security payments, annuities, trusts, and any other sources. Add the assessed value of your home(s) and furnishings, and such personal property as automobiles and valuable jewelry, art, and other collectibles.

Now list your annual expenses. Referring to your tax returns and worksheets, bank statements, and appointment calendars will be necessary.

This expenses checklist includes the most common items, but it is by no means all-inclusive.

- rent or mortgage
- personal, property, and other taxes
- insurance (including health insurance)
- loans, including mortgages, interest payments, and carrying charges
- ascertainable medical expenses, including any future ones (e.g., a surgical procedure that you know you'll need down the road)
- gas, water, electricity, and other utilities
- telephone (including mobile phones), TV cable service, and computer ISP charges
- membership fees
- cost of gardening, indoor cleaning services, and caregiving services
- transportation (the cost of operating your car(s), including garage rental if one doesn't come with your home, and/or public transportation)

- food and drink (if you can't figure out how much you spend annually on, for example, groceries and other in-home eats and drinks, compute an average week's costs; then multiply by 52)
- tobacco
- medications and other pharmaceuticals
- personal items and grooming (clothing, laundry, makeup, and haircut/hairdresser, manicure)
- sports equipment and fees
- pet care and supplies
- entertainment (including season tickets and subscriptions)
- vacations
- charitable contributions
- gratuities (e.g., end-of-year tips)

After you compute the bottom line of your assets and liabilities come the payoff questions: What is your short- and long-term financial health? Will your money indeed last as long as you do?

For the most accurate estimation of and strategy for your monetary survival, both pre- and postretirees find life easier by using the services of a financial planner. That person might be your accountant or stockbroker, both of whom are familiar with your wealth and your lifestyle. If you do your own taxes and handle your own investment portfolio, ask for a recommendation from your lawyer, especially if he or she is associated with an elder-law specialist. Friends or relatives, especially those who have gone the route themselves, may know of someone. If you are retiring on good terms with your employer, the company's human resources department may be able to make a suggestion.

Anyone looking on her or his own should be aware that some advisors represent themselves as "certified senior planners" or "registered retirement financial specialists" without having valid credentials. You'd be far better off going through established and reliable national organizations whose members earned their credentials through qualifying exams and whose websites will lead to members in the state where you live. These organizations (and their websites) include The American Institute of Certified Public Accountants [aicpa.org], the National Association of Personal Financial Advisors [napfa.org], the Financial Planning Association [plannersearch.org], and the Certified Financial Planner Board of Standards [cfp.net]. As you interview any likely candidates, you'll want to look for someone who's experienced, with whom you find a strong comfort level, and whose preliminary questions show a supportive understanding of your situation.

Once you've found such an individual or team, you and they will create a plan that will include optimizing assets management, minimizing tax liabilities, repaying outstanding loans, keeping up with inflation, and otherwise making retirement years as financially comfortable as possible.

* * * * * *

With or without professional assistance, you may well discover to your dismay that your nest egg's present bottom line and future projections are less rosy than anticipated or desired. If so, a strategy that you can do on your own is find and take advantage of interesting and satisfying alternatives to more expensive activities. Granted, it's belt-tightening, a phase that if you find depressing, try to think of it less as contracting your life and more as a way to expand your horizons.

A lifelong baseball fan named Tim who lives in a Midwestern city was dismayed that season tickets to his hometown's major league team had spiraled above his budget. So had the cost of stadium parking, programs, and refreshments (and hey, what's a ball game without hot dogs and a beer?). Sure, he could have given up the season pass in favor of going to a few games, but that would have meant scrambling for the equivalent good seats he had for years. Instead, he'd watch the season on TV and be done with it.

A friend who was also retired talked Tim into spending an afternoon at a Triple A minor league game in a nearby town. Despite his

reservations, Tim found himself thoroughly enjoying the eagerness of rookie players on their way up and the professionalism of older players, as well as the chance to watch a major leaguer who was there to recuperate from an injury. Tim found himself chuckling at such between-inning promotions as a madcap run-the-bases race among Mr. Mustard, Mr. Ketchup, and Mr. Relish. Moreover, a ticket for a very good seat, parking, and snacks were a bargain compared to what he had been spending. The first game led to others, and Tim became hooked.

A decade ago a husband and wife who live in a large East Coast city were accustomed to going out to dinner several times a week. Once they both retired, they became more aware of where their discretionary funds were going and realized to their shock and chagrin that several favorite restaurants had become above their budgetary comfort level ("all the spaghetti you can eat for $300" was how the husband described one such place). In addition to cutting back on the fancy eateries, they started exploring other restaurants, especially those offering unfamiliar cuisines. Using suggestions from newspaper and magazine reviews, they went out to lunch at, among others, Thai, Ethiopian, Spanish, and Southern "soul food" places, returning another day for dinner at the ones they liked.

Once they became known as regulars, the owners and staff offered "off the menu" suggestions. Doing research into the cuisines and the cultures from which they came added to the couple's appreciation. When vacation time came, they gave up their customary trip to a golf resort in favor of ten days in Spain, their itinerary based on cities and towns recommended by "their" restaurant's owner. And, as a special treat, unbeknownst to the couple, the owner had gotten in touch with friends, and the couple was received and treated royally wherever they went.

Here's one more example. Instead of renewing costly opera and symphony subscriptions, a New York City couple started attending faculty and graduate student recitals and performances at Julliard and other music schools. Chatting with other attendees during intermission, they learned of other free or low-cost, high-level opportunities, a musical panorama that expanded their knowledge and appreciation.

* * * * * *

Plan Ahead

Amid the optimism of expanding one's retirement horizons, an unavoidable cloud on that horizon is that we're not getting any younger. Therefore, while considering the financial side of the pasture, give thought to estate planning.

Estate planning is the process of organizing your financial and personal assets so that when that inevitable event occurs, your wishes can be carried out with a minimum of inconvenience and expense. "Inconvenience" can include going through the probate system, and in that regard there are many ways to reduce assets that probate will consider. Indeed, there are ways to avoid probate entirely. As for the expense side, estate planning can ensure that any estate that is subject to estate tax will incur the minimum possible liability.

Making a Will

If you don't have a Will (uppercase W for clarity), you should with very few exceptions rectify that omission as soon as you can. People without a Will die what's called intestate, lawyer-talk for "Will-less." State and federal laws then dictate who is entitled to your property, and your assets may end up going to people you'd be unhappy to see benefitting that way.

How complicated your Will will be depends on what you have and what you want to do with it. Although there are "do-it-yourself" books and computer programs that will guide you through the procedure, you might still value the peace of mind of knowing that your lawyer made sure the document's consequences will be exactly what you wish.

In general, the Testator—the person making the Will—should have the mental capacity to understand what his property's value is, which of his beneficiaries will get what property, and how rational the plan of distribution will be. (To cite an extreme example, a testator's wanting to leave everything to "that cute little red-head I had a crush on in grammar school if I could only remember her name after all these years" would raise serious doubts about the testator's competency.) The idea is to protect unhappy heirs from claiming more than their designated shares, or a person unmentioned in the Will trying to nullify the document. If there's even the slightest chance of raising the issue of senility or insanity, lawyers often videotape Will-signings, during which time the Testator is questioned about the Will's contents, his family, other beneficiaries, and other key provisions.

A typical simple Will begins with your name and a declaration that what you're executing is indeed your Last Will and Testament. Such language as "bequeath, convey, and devise" that is found in many Wills may seem stilted or quaint, but the words have definite legal consequences, the reason why they continue to be used. Then comes a paragraph about paying your creditors, followed by specific bequests (lawyer-talk for gifts), and then directions about the disposition of the remainder of the estate (that is, everything else after your specific bequests). There will also be a paragraph appointing your executor or personal representative, and one about payment of taxes. There may also be something about providing for minor children or incapacitated adults, and even beloved pets.

That's basically all that's needed in a simple Will, but since life is rarely simple, other provisions might include your wishes about your burial or cremation and any organ donation.

A testamentary trust, which is a trust included in and created by a Will, can be a sensible addition. Unlike a living trust, property conveyed by a testamentary trust is subject to the court-involved probate process. That's because testamentary trusts are usually intended primarily to keep large sums of money from immediately passing to children or other next-of-kin who need assistance managing money. A designated trustee is appointed to administer the funds on behalf of the beneficiaries usually until they reach a certain age.

Although most states require two witnesses to a Will, others want three. Choosing witnesses who are not named as a beneficiary or an Executor (the person who supervises distribution under the Will) makes sense in order to avoid any potential or alleged conflict of interest. Your lawyer will choreograph such details.

How frequently your Will should be reviewed with an eye to changing any of its provisions depends on your and your family's situation. Marriage or divorce, the birth of a child or a grandchild, and the death of any beneficiary would be reason enough. So would a beneficiary's falling out of favor or experiencing changed circumstances. Case in point: if you've left a legacy to a needy relative who later hits the lottery for big bucks, you might want to give the legacy to someone else (and hope that Mr. Lucky remembers you in his Will).

Even if there hasn't been any such a signal event, lawyers and estate planners often suggest reviewing the document every five years; just looking at the provisions may give you pause for reflection and possible action.

* * * * * *

Although you have a Will, there are ways to keep many, if not all, of your assets out of your estate, even in ways that will not require your executor ever to have to file the Will for probate. That is to say, savvy estate planning can provide your beneficiaries with your assets by other means.

Unlike a testamentary trust, a living trust (also called an *inter vivos* trust, from the Latin for "among the living") is one that's created when the settler (lawyer-talk for the trust-creator but sometimes called the grantor) is alive. It's a very useful mechanism that allows your assets to be distributed easily and quickly after your death without making use of the often lengthy and expensive probate process. It's frequently used when privacy is a consideration; a living trust isn't registered with or revealed in a probate court. And if for any reason you become incapacitated, a living trust can authorize someone else to manage your affairs, or at least those elements that are included in the trust.

Although the trust legally owns the property, you needn't relinquish control if you don't want to. You can appoint yourself to be the trustee (the person who administers the trust), which gives you authority over whatever was placed in trust. You can add to or sell all of it or just parts, such as real estate (including time shares), businesses (entire or your portion of the ownership), investment securities, or works of art. And since at some point you might change your mind about the whole idea, you can create a revocable trust that's terminable whenever you wish.

There are, however, limitations to living trusts, and your lawyer can explain which items can or can't and should or shouldn't be placed in one, as well as tax consequences and life events when your trust should be reviewed. Estate planners recommend that you include an "incapacity" clause to permit a trustee to manage your affairs should you become physically or mentally unable to do so.

Also, while looking toward the future, a Power of Attorney for Health Care and a Living Will to cover medical considerations, especially matters of life and death, would also be a good thing to have.

You may already have existing arrangements by which assets will be transferred at death. They include IRAs and 401(k)s, stocks, bonds and other securities, insurance policies, and bank accounts where you've indicated who is to receive the proceeds after your death. Another technique is a joint tenancy whereby two or more people acquire property (and not just real estate) together. Joint tenancies confer the right of survivorship whereby the deceased's interests pass to the survivors. The marital equivalent is called tenancy by the entirety; the surviving spouse acquires the property by operation of law.

To find and use an estate planner to preserve your assets and then to know that they will be distributed according to your wishes is both responsible and essential. Why (if you've not realized by now)? Because, as Ben Franklin reflected, "In this world nothing can be said to be certain, except death and taxes."

* * * * * *

If thinking about estate matters makes you shudder, here comes an even grimmer subject. Although no one likes to contemplate death, especially his or her own, the event will happen, and sometimes sooner than anticipated. That's why estate planning should also include other ways to make the tasks of surviving relatives and friends as uncomplicated as possible.

What would you like done with your remains—burial or cremation? If the former, have you selected a cemetery? If the latter, what would you like done with your ashes? Talk to your spouse or partner and children (if any), or a close friend or your lawyer if you're unattached. If you want to be interred and you've no particular cemetery in mind, choosing one that will make visitations easy for your survivors is a thoughtful gesture; or let them choose. You might also want to investigate prepaid funeral contracts.

Also give thought to the sort of funeral or memorial service you'd like to have, if you in fact want one. Whom would you like to officiate and whom would you like to speak? Are there meaningful poetry verses, prose excerpts, and/or music you care to be read or played? Discuss the matter with your spouse or partner and/or children before it's too late, or else leave the details in a letter if the subject is too sensitive to talk about.

To be sure, death is an uninviting subject, but, like taxes, it's unavoidable and emotionally painful, and a well-planned estate is a gift that will survive your passing.

4

MAKING A MOVE: POSTRETIREMENT RELOCATING

"Time is a circus, always packing up and moving away."
—Ben Hecht

While you're deciding how you want to reinvent yourself, you might consider the question of *where* you want to do it.

That question may seem the height of irrelevance to retirees who have lived in the same village, town, or city since birth—indeed, some people have lived in the same apartment or house all their lives. If you're one of them, you probably can't come up with any compelling reason to move. You own your house or apartment free and clear, your roots are in the community, as are your friends and relatives, and wanderlust is not part of your makeup. Even thinking about the hassle of getting new return-address stickers for your envelopes seems overwhelming.

However, even if Hometown, USA, will be forever in your heart, there may be convincing reasons to relocate.

Life in suburban or rural areas was much easier when you were younger. You didn't think twice about driving to restaurants, shopping centers, recreation facilities, doctors' offices, and cultural attractions or to visit friends. But with age comes a diminution of energy. A forty-minute drive each way to save money by shopping at a Costco or Sam's Club now seems more and more of a chore, especially in inclement weather. You also find that your tolerance for traffic jams and other inconveniences is less than what it had been.*

Convenience or the lack of it became an issue in my family. When they were in their fifties, my mother-in-law and her second husband bought a weekend house in a small town a three-hour drive north of New York City. They liked the house and the area so much that when they both retired from the travel industry in their late sixties, they gave up their Manhattan apartment in favor of rural life.

The relocation worked well for the first dozen or so years. A gregarious sort, my mother-in-law became active in local politics, the library, and a play-reading group. She had her weekly bridge game. An outdoorsy and DIY type, her husband filled his days gardening, fishing, building birdhouses in a basement workshop, visiting with neighbors, and making home repairs. They were never at a loss for things that were mentally and physically stimulating things to do.

Until, that is, my mother-in-law suffered a foot injury. Following surgery, and perhaps because of an adverse reaction to the anesthesia (as often happens with elderly patients), she developed memory loss that led to dementia, a life-altering event. The combination of my mother-in-law's condition and both her and her husband's aging made their children and grandchildren wish the couple wasn't so reliant on his driving ability, and they regretted his refusal to sell the house. Moving back to New York City or another urban area would put them in an environment where shopping, medical facilities, and home health care were easily accessible by public transportation, taxis, or walking.

---

*On the other hand, metropolitan living isn't always every city-dweller's idea of a retirement dream. An AARP survey of New York City's voters age fifty and older revealed that more than half plan to leave the city when they retire.

And when the weather or physical limitations would make leaving an apartment inadvisable, virtually everything that any urbanite would want or need can be delivered. But no, that's not going to happen.

The moral of this tale: hope for the best, but plan for the worst.

* * * * * *

Downsizing

You're sitting around the house that you've occupied for many years. Your spouse asks you to fetch something that's in another part of the house. To get it requires a long hike involving flights of stairs. You pass unoccupied rooms that haven't been used since your children left and that now lie fallow behind closed doors. You get the item, retrace your steps, and, once back, you look across the room at your spouse, who looks inquiringly back at you as you proclaim, "I for one have had enough of rattling around this old barn!"

Another scenario involves increasing hardship in navigating around a large residence, although not to the point of needing an assisted living facility. Then, too, changing financial circumstances may make your present home too expensive to maintain. But whatever the reason, you decide the time to downsize has come.

The simplest way in terms of logistics is giving up the old homestead in favor a smaller one in your hometown or the same city. Even without a medical or financial reason, it's a way to uncomplicate your life: less space to pay for and keep clean. There's also the opportunity to sell the place for a profit and then buy a smaller one that requires less time, money, and effort to maintain, all the while remaining in a familiar area with old friends and other roots and attachments to the community.

Unlike the days of your upwardly mobile youth when you yearned for as much space as you could afford, you're now looking for only as much room as you need and can manage. If it's an apartment you want, a two-bedroom suite should suffice for a couple who would use

the spare bedroom as a den/guest room. Otherwise, a two-bedroom townhouse or small ranch house would serve the same purpose.

By the same token, the real estate mantra "location! location! location!" must be expanded to include "convenience! convenience! convenience!" Accessibility is an essential element in where you will garage your car if you plan to keep it and your new home has no parking facilities. Easy access to public transportation and stores that carry essential items is equally important, since moving to a place where you must spend time and effort getting to and from frequently visited destinations makes little sense. "Convenience" in the case of an apartment building also means a doorman who accepts deliveries, a superintendent who lives on the premises, and a porter/handyman who'll do chores and make repairs that you can't.

In the event that you use a real estate agent, the agent must understand all your requirements. In that regard, a category of realtors specializes in exactly the issues that you are facing. They're called Senior Real Estate Specialists; see www.seniorsrealestate.com, and, as an article in *The New York Times* described them, the ones who have qualified for this designation are "part therapist, part housekeeper, part business advisor, and part diplomat."

"Why would I need a therapist and a diplomat?" you may wonder. That's because older people who relocate are faced with many emotional challenges. You'll be saying goodbye to familiar surroundings with their memories of major events in your life—you'll find that even just thinking about leaving gives rise to waves of nostalgia. Tangible evidence of these surroundings and events are the possessions you acquired over the years, but here's another grabber: you can't take them all with you when you move.

Nor would you want to. Some items are easily left behind or relegated to Goodwill or the flames: a lawnmower you won't need in your new apartment, the shoebox full of 1983 income tax receipts stored in the back of a closet shelf behind that pair of shoes you haven't worn in decades, the chafing dish last used during the 1960s fondue party craze, or a souvenir program from a rock 'n' roll concert that neither you nor your spouse remembers attending.

However, how about that manila folder of your daughter's kindergarten drawings and the wallet your son made for you at summer camp? The photo of your great-grandfather? Your college economics textbook, your fraternity ring, or a dusty anthology of Elizabeth Barrett Browning poems you cherished during your teenage years?

Weeding through furniture, clothing, and other possessions isn't nearly so easy as you might have thought. Your child or another relative helping you may not make the task any easier, since they're likely to seize on an item with a mournful "But, Mom, you can't throw *that* balsam-scented pillow away—remember, we got it when we took that wonderful family vacation to Gitche Gumee."

Here's where another specialist can come to the rescue. Members of the National Association of Senior Move Managers [www.nasmm. org] are experienced in helping you with the daunting triage task of deciding between what you should take with you and what you should dispose of via sale, donation, or trashcan. An alternative to Senior Move Managers might be your real estate broker if he or she has the time and interest. If not, the realtor may know of someone who'd be happy to work with you for a fee.

In the meantime, experts suggest that you begin this downsizing process as soon as you decide to move. The physical side of packing and moving is stressful (some would call it traumatic) enough without having a nostalgia cloud hanging over your head too.

* * * * * *

Many older people with close family ties think about moving nearer to their children and grandchildren. That's especially true when sons and daughters and their own children once lived nearby and close bonds developed among the generations, but then employment relocation caused a geographic separation. You can imagine the following conversation taking place during the plane ride home from visiting the kids over Christmas holidays:

"George, isn't it hard to believe how the grand-babies have grown since we saw them over the summer? Karla is taking a dance class and is making her debut in a few weeks. What a shame we'll miss it."

"It is. But they're not such babies anymore. Mikey is active in student government and clubs and teams. Before I know it, he'll be too busy to want to take any more fishing trips with me."

"Honey, we wouldn't miss seeing them grow up if we moved out there. There's nothing tying us to where we live now . . ."

"You have a point, Martha. And we can find tons of things to do when we're not with the kids. There's got to be a library that needs your volunteer help. And didn't someone mention a retired executive mentoring program like the one I do at home?"

"Right you are, George. Tell you what, let's search the Internet for real estate brokers. In the meantime, we can start placing our home on the market. And let's not tell the kids till we find a new place to live—we'll make it a real surprise!"

Commenting on the above scenario, grandparents and parents called it a recipe for disaster. First of all, taking such a major step so impulsively leaves you open to inherent problems. What if you can't sell your old house or condo/co-op or get out of the lease of your present apartment without taking a huge loss or paying a sizable penalty? What if you can't immediately find a new residence to your liking? Are you willing to settle for "any old place" and spend additional time looking for a better apartment or house? And what if your children who moved away because of job relocation are obliged to move yet again? Would you be willing to stay in your new area without them, or are you prepared to move again?

More fundamental is the possibility that even though your children think they live in paradise, you may not like your new surroundings' climate, politics, lack of culture, and other unappealing aspects. What if, after living there for a while, you conclude that the proximity to your kids and grandkids isn't enough?

Speaking of whom, the biggest mistake you can make is to withhold your "surprise" from your children. Much as they love you, they may have settled into new routines that would leave little time for you. Sure, your grandkids would be delighted to have you around, at least up until they grow up, but their parents may see having their own parents in the same community as—let's face facts—a liability. Although, to put it crassly, they're grateful for a free and reliable babysitting service, they may feel obligated to include you in their parties and other occasions where your presence would make everyone feel comfortable. Then, too, as your medical problems develop over time, your children may not be happy to become your primary caregivers. In light of the above reservations, you'd do well to offer them the chance to discuss your move between themselves first and then with you at a "family council" so they can have a say in the matter.

All right then, let's say that your children have no objections to your relocating to their city or town. In fact, they think it's a great idea (so do your other adult children because you made sure to check with them to avoid hurt feelings). They may be so happy that, assuming they live in a dwelling and on a property large enough to allow expansion, they suggest moving in with them. This arrangement is also suitable if you and your children already live in the same area. If all of you do decide to share a residence, you'll be part of a growing number of multigenerational families under one roof. The total number of Americans with this living arrangement has reached 56.8 million, nearly 18 percent of the population. Although almost half are working parents and "boomerang" grown children who can't afford to live on their own, nearly as many arrangements consist of three generations or more. In fact, 20 percent of Americans age sixty-five or older live in multigenerational households. But having a parent or two move in is a big physical, financial, and emotional adjustment for all concerned, and it is important to be prepared.

Consider the physical area. Will you live in a spare bedroom and share a bathroom, or a suite with its own bath, or will you have an entire floor? Is there a separate cottage or guesthouse on the property? Or will an addition to the house be necessary? Must the driveway be widened to accommodate another car, and/or will a new carport or larger garage be part of the renovations? With regard to privacy, a separate entrance is widely considered to be the most important feature of a two-family dwelling.

The new living space must be elder-friendly. Even if you can now manage in a "younger" environment, someday you won't. For example, although you may now be as nimble as a mountain goat, climbing flights of steep steps will at some point become an issue. (A checklist of items and features in the appendix offers many suggestions in this regard.)

With regard to finances, who will pay for the physical improvements is a crucial question. Even if money is no object to your children, your paying in full or in part gives you both a financial and an emotional equity. If you have other children, they may be asked to contribute even though you won't be living with them. There is also the matter of how much you can or should contribute to the cost of food and utilities. Most experts agree that contributing to the cost of food, utilities, and other household expenses makes a parent feel less like a guest and more like a full member of the home.

Tax consequences may come into play once a dwelling or property is improved. Parents who contribute to the renovation may want to convey their portion of the equity to their children or retain an interest or put it in a trust (which option you choose may affect Medicaid eligibility if moving to a nursing home ever becomes necessary). A lawyer and/or accountant who specializes in elder-care matters can advise you and your children about these and related matters.

Tolstoy began *Anna Karenina* with the observation, "All happy families are alike; each unhappy family is unhappy in its own way." That would include intergenerational friction that can run rampant in families who live together unless ground rules are firmly established and adhered to.

First and foremost, privacy is paramount, although *sacred* may be a better word. That's especially important if everyone is sharing the same apartment or common living quarters in the same house. Not to barge into another's room or suite intentionally or inadvertently and not to borrow another's possession without permission may seem so basic it's not worth saying, but space-sharers will tell you that it happens. If everyone in the house takes certain meals together, alert the food preparer well in advance if your plans change. Or if the arrangement calls for you to use the kitchen and eat first but something delays your getting home in time, let everyone know.

Noise-sharing is another point that may seem insignificant in theory, but loud music (especially the kind you don't like) or blaring TV sound coming through walls is grounds for complaint. As with other "minor" points, don't suffer in silence until you reach the screaming point.

Like contributing financially, pitching in to do chores makes you part of the household. You may love to cook and will eagerly take on that task. You may not mind dusting and vacuuming or doing laundry and then ironing whatever needs to be ironed. Walking the dog can be your thing even in lousy weather. However, there'll come a time when you may not physically be able to carry out your assigned chores, and everyone should be aware of and acknowledge that reassignments will become necessary.

The solution to all such problems is simple "golden rule" courtesy without which resentment begins by gnawing until, unresolved, it explodes into unhappy situations. You may have encountered similar thoughtlessness and friction with a college roommate who became so intolerable that one or the other of you felt obliged to change rooms and roommates. However, that was then and this is now: such options are no longer available unless you choose to pack up and move out, something likely to lead to ill-will that will infect your family and will last for a long time, if not forever.

Parents who move into their children's home must acknowledge that they no longer rule the roost. Although your word might have been law "back in the day," it no longer is. That's particularly true when it comes to dealing with your grandchildren. They may have been little angels when they were younger, but bear in mind the feuding-fussing-and-fighting when your own kids reached an age where they asserted their sense of self and independence. That will happen again, but this time around you're strictly a spectator (although possibly, but only with your children's acquiescence, a mediator or court of last resort).

That's not to say there won't be times when opportunities to become involved are minefields of danger. For example, you know that your grandson has an important French test coming up and that he's weak in conjugating irregular verbs. The night before the exam you see him doing everything but studying. Do you tell him to put away the video game and hit the books? And if you do, what if he talks back to you, and in language you consider entirely inappropriate? Or your adolescent granddaughter is hanging out with friends whom you consider to be disreputable. Do you sit her down for a stern lecture or do you tattle to her parents? Or do you keep quiet? The decision is yours, but the consequences affect all in the family. That's why it's far better to include such scenarios in pre-move discussions with your children, if not with the entire clan.

* * * * * *

Community Living

What comes to mind when you hear the phrase "retirement home"? Ancient frail residents in wheelchairs or pushing walkers aimlessly up and down antiseptic-looking (and smelling) corridors? Seniors sitting around card tables, playing shuffleboard, or showing photographs of grandchildren?

Although that might have been the stereotypical image decades ago, retirement residences are now a far cry from "Death's waiting rooms." Thanks to the needs and wishes of the rapidly growing population of seniors and aging boomers, a range of facilities offer lifestyles that rival and often surpass what their residents had been accustomed to. Even the phrase "retirement home" is passé because of its passive-sounding connotation. Retirement homes are now called "community living" or "independent living."

"Independent living" refers to housing designed exclusively for seniors, roughly defined as those aged fifty-five and over. It ranges from apartment-style living where rent may include meals in a communal dining area to groups of detached housing units known as a senior community whose membership fees can include maintenance of the building and grounds and recreation and social facilities.

Living where you live now is fine when help that you hire to help with daily chores is adequate, but if you or your spouse needs special assistance in carrying out creature comforts or for ongoing medical aid, an assisted living facility would be more appropriate. It offers a continuum of help: the individual or the spouse who is fully independent carries on daily life as always, but when someone needs medical care, that person moves to a location within the facility. You or your spouse may not need such care now, but think of it the way you think about insurance: you don't need it till you need it, but when you need it, it's nice to know it's there.

Making the decision to choose this category of living arrangement is not easy. You may be in excellent physical health. Although your present abode is getting harder to maintain, or there's too much unused space, it's still the home-sweet-home that you're loathe to leave. Friends are moving away or unable to socialize as they once did or—let's face it—dying. You're trying to talk yourself into believing that loneliness is now a fact of life.

Now look at your situation with some perspective. Maintaining a residence becomes burdensome with age. Although full- or part-time hired help, if you can afford it, will solve many problems, even then you may one day find yourself stranded if the helper leaves or ages out. Also with age comes diminished mobility, which involves more than negotiating staircases or walking in inclement weather. Driving becomes a hassle or downright dangerous, a limitation on your getting out and about to activities that you enjoy, which increases feelings of loneliness. On the other hand, independent living facilities offer built-in social networks of real live human beings, not just via phone or Facebook. Special-interest facilities that focus on sports and the arts (participatory or spectator), religious affiliation, or other interests will keep you engaged to whatever extent you choose.

Cost is also an element. The average annual charge of an assisted-living facility is $34,000, and it can be more twice that figure in expensive metropolitan areas. Another factor to consider is your or your spouse's health. A specific medical condition that will worsen with time invites you and your loved one to think about when you or he or she can no longer provide the necessary care. To be able to move to a friendly and familiar part of the facility will lighten the physical and emotional loads that you will bear.

Locating a Residence

Word-of-mouth is a good place to start when it comes to finding places to look at. If medical assistance for you or a spouse is required, your physician can often offer recommendations. Otherwise, ask relatives and friends, and ask them to ask relatives and friends. The wider the pool of people who know you or know about you, the more likely their suggestions will have been prescreened ("Aw, he/she/they wouldn't like the place"). Especially helpful will be people you know through activities. If you're a golfer, someone at the club or course may know someone who retired to a links-linked facility and who's happy with the decision. If you're a volunteer at a local museum, someone on the staff may tell you about a former curator who's involved with a museum near the residence to which he or she retired that's always looking for help. Or you're an amateur musician—someone with whom you play or jam says he or she knows a player who knows a player who's living somewhere where there's a resident string quartet/jazz/bluegrass/ blues/rock band.

Sound tempting? That's the way to get names of people to get in touch with for further information and whom you can visit if and when you inspect the facility.

Newspapers and magazines provide additional sources for leads. Look for ads in AARP's *Modern Maturity* and other magazines that focus on senior or about-to-be-senior citizens. Golf, tennis, and other sports periodicals have retirement community ads on a regular basis, as do almost every college and university alumni magazine.

The Internet has hundreds of websites to help you find a place to live. Some are listed in the footnotes herein. For others, use a search engine: "retirement communities" + geographic area + any other specifics, such as "pet-friendly" or "gardening opportunities" or "fishing" or "art museums."*

Also to be found in ads and on the web are free services that will help you locate a facility. These services, it may not surprise you to learn, receive a fee from those facilities to which the services successfully steer clients. Although they're not presenting the entire retirement-home universe, there's no harm in contacting them.**

The facility will provide a guided tour, and, although the guide's sales pitch will cover all the essential points, questions to ask, plus ones to ask yourself, include the following:

Location: Is the facility in a safe and clean area or neighborhood? Are the grounds pleasant and easy to walk around? Are food shopping, banking facilities, restaurants, and such other amenities as a barbershop or hairdresser within easy access, whether by your own car, the facility's bus or jitney service, and/or public transportation?

The Facility Itself: First impressions are important. Are the buildings and grounds clean and well maintained? Do they feel inviting? In short, is it a place where you'd enjoy living? Are the rooms/suites/apartments also clean and well maintained? Are the furniture and fixtures in furnished rooms senior-friendly (and can you bring in your own furniture and furnishings)? Are there any curfews or noise restrictions?

Are hallways and common areas equally safe and inviting? How close are communal dining and recreation areas to living areas? Are there facilities for private family gatherings, and, if so, can special meals be supplied or brought in? Is there adequate parking for residents and guests?

---

*When it comes time to inspect a prospect, make an appointment with the sales department even if you know someone who lives there.

** The initial phone call or email is also the time for pet owners to inquire whether Fido or Mittens will be welcome.

Dining: If you plan to be on a meal plan, ask to have a lunch or dinner there. Are the food and its presentation (table settings and table arrangement) to your liking? What times are meals served, and is there any flexibility in case your schedule conflicts with meal hours? Will you receive credit for missed meals?

Ask to see a week's menu: Does it suit your taste, and, if not, are substitutes available? Are dietary restrictions honored? Are snacks available at all reasonable hours? Can meals be delivered to your living quarters? Can guests be accommodated? If so, how many and at what additional charge?

Staff: Do staff members appear attentive to residents' wants/needs? Do they seem to take the initiative whenever they see a reason to help, or do they wait to be asked? Do members of the staff have special training (as in emergency medical assistance) or credentials? Is the medical care sufficient for your or your spouse's present and anticipated future needs? How available are maintenance people when a resident's fixtures or appliances must be repaired or replaced?

A useful adjunct at some places are "senior helpers" (a reference not to their age but to whom they assist). Paid at hourly or day rates, these staff members or outsiders can best be thought of as "temporary assisted-caregivers." Case in point: an otherwise physically capable husband who pushes his wife in a wheelchair for after-dinner strolls around the grounds used their services following his own surgery until he was able to resume the activity

Pets: Many facilities allow residents to move in with their dogs, cats, and birds, but do not allow acquiring new animals (newcomers may be too disorderly until they settle in). There may also be such limitations as unruly or menacing dogs or ones whose barking disturbs neighbors. If you own a pet that will join you, you'll want to know whether staff members can look after Rover, Tabby, or Polly while you're away for a day or two. And for any longer absences, you'll want the name of a convenient veterinarian or boarding kennel.

Activities: How wide is the range of activities—for instance, a bridge club, literary discussion/book club, film club, art studio instruction (with or without "gallery" exhibitions), current events discussion group, orchestra or band, amateur theatricals/drama group—and how often do they meet? Ask yourself how many of these social and cultural events are the kinds in which you'd enjoy taking part. Is there ready access to "off-campus" activities in which you'd be interested? Are fitness programs available, such as a gym and/or swimming pool, with trained staff in attendance (including a lifeguard if there's a pool)? Do specialized on-site sports such as golf or tennis require lengthy waits for playing time and/or extra fees?

Continuity of Care: This feature of a multipurpose retirement residence may prove to be the most important either now or at some point in your or your spouse's life. How long or short are the waiting periods, from an independent living residence to an assisted living unit and from either to a continuing care unit? What is the on-site availability of doctors, and what are their specialties? Are such doctors available to become your primary care physician should you need one? Is there access to skilled nursing care?

Cost: What are the financial requirements (income, savings, investments) to live in the facility? Is there a membership bond or another form of entry payment? If a membership facility, would moving into a full-time assisted living section be at a reduced rate?

Would you purchase or rent your residence? If purchase, are there any resale restrictions? What is the total monthly rental or maintenance fee? Are there fixed increases (typically an annual cost-of-living increase)? Does a resident council or another representative group oversee the increases? Have there been any anticipated extraordinary pass-along expenses? What are the hidden fees or extras, such as staff gratuities? What are the consequences of your becoming unable to afford living there?

In addition to the above questions dealing with initial and ongoing costs, you'll want to ask about matters that the facility's representatives might be reluctant to discuss. You wouldn't buy a house with a weak foundation, and, by the same token, you want to be certain that the facility's financial underpinnings are up to the task. Some facilities either began with or incurred severe difficulties along the way, like undercapitalization, foreclosed units, or financially delinquent residents, all of which are likely to require assessments from their present residents. Ask for whatever financial statements a prospective resident is entitled to see and, if appropriate, condominium or homeowner association meeting minutes. Unless you're a lawyer or an accountant, ask your professionals to review and comment on the documents.

It may be love at first sight and all your questions are answered to your satisfaction, but if you are not ready to commit and you think the facility has potential, plan to return for a closer and more informed inspection. See whether you can take part in an activity or two. You'll have a chance to get a feeling for the ambiance and to meet residents who, over a meal or during a stroll around the premises, can share insights and experiences that you won't get from brochures, financial statements, or interviews with facility administrators.

And if it's not love at first or second sight, you'll have developed skills that will help you find your dream destination.

As a starting point, retirenet.com, 55places.com, privatecommunities.com, retirementcommunities.com, and seniorhomes.com all offer interactive information about retirement, assisted living, and rehabilitation facilities across the United States.

* * * * * *

Back To School

A growing number of retirees, not just the academically inclined, are relocating to college towns. Although the primary attraction is a rich intellectual and cultural milieu, seniors have discovered that youthful energies that infuse college towns are stimuli for their own physical and social well-being.

Not just any city or town with one or more junior college, colleges, or universities qualifies. New York City, Boston, and Washington, DC, have dozens of schools, but you wouldn't call them college towns even if certain sections may look and sound that way on Saturday nights. In *Choose a College Town for Retirement: Retirement Discoveries for Every Budget*, author Joe Lubow points out criteria that retirees should use: at least one school in the area is a major focus of community life; at least one school must offer educational and cultural opportunities to adults, preferably a program aimed to seniors; the school or the city or town itself organizes events in which the population participates and interacts, such as concerts in the park or holiday celebrations; and the school and/or the community offers frequent opportunities for nonstudents to attend museums, concerts, lectures, sports, and other events. These points are in addition to other features that a prospective resident would find appealing: a safe and attractive environment, adequate medical facilities, and easy access to transportation and shopping.

Having fond memories of your bright college years doesn't necessarily mean that moving back to your alma mater is right for you. The city or town may well have changed over the decades, and the school may have changed. You have too—you might have been a Big Man on Campus or the Homecoming Queen back then, but no one at the fraternity or sorority house now cares. Similarly, just because you drove through a charming college town close to a favorite ski resort or vacationed near one that had a terrific summer stock theater is hardly a reason in itself to pull up roots and settle down there.

Once again, it's up to you to do your due diligence. Ask around. For example, if the school in which you're interested is affiliated with the religious denomination to which you belong, find out whether your clergymen and -women know anything about the school's current reputation. When you visit—and an extended stay of at least one month is highly advisable—consult local newspapers and especially the school's student paper for a realistic overview of activities. The school's web-site will indicate seminars, courses, lectures, and other activities open to and aimed at senior scholars, and you should be able to audit one or two while you're visiting. If you think entering a degree program is something you might do—and many seniors do—ask about tuition discounts for seniors. If that sounds as if you're applying to the school, in a real sense you are, since the area's campus life will become an integral part of your own life.

Want to surround yourself with fellow alumni of the school you attended? A number of schools have independent-living or continuing-care residences either on campus or nearby. Among them are:

- Anderson University, Anderson, IN. University Village Condominiums
- University of Arizona, Tucson, AZ. The Academy Village
- University of Central Arkansas, Conway, AR. College Square
- Ithaca College, NY. Longview
- Lasell College, Newton, MA. Lasell Village
- University of Michigan, Ann Arbor, MI. University Commons
- Notre Dame, Sound Bend, IN. Holy Cross Village
- University of Florida, Oak Hammock, FL
- Penn State University, State College, PA. The Village at Penn State
- University of Florida, Gainesville, FL. Oak Hammock
- The Forest at Duke, Durham, NC
- Rochester Institute of Technology, Rochester, NY. Rivers Run

Others can be found at the Best Guide retirement communities website: www.bestguide-retirementcommunities.com/Collegelinked-retirementcommunities.html. You can find out from your alma mater if yours has any such facilities, if you haven't already seen ads in alumni magazines.

Realizing that retirees are growth industry, Institutes for Learning in Retirement offers programs that are administered at colleges but are conducted by the institute members who design courses led by the school's faculty, by other experts, or by the members of the group itself. See www.roadscholar.org/ein/map_usca.asp for a list.

Similarly, the Bernard Osher Foundation sponsors adult education opportunities at more than one hundred colleges and universities [www.osherfoundation.org/index.php?olli]. Even if you're not planning to relocate, taking advantage of a continuing education program in your area might be of interest.

* * * * * *

After the brutal northern winter of 2013–14, the idea of becoming a permanent snowbird in sunnier climes has become increasingly appealing. Although hurricanes trouble the Gulf States and droughts are an ever-present problem in the Southwest, as your friends who now live in those parts of the country are fond of reminding you, you don't have to shovel rain or sunshine.

Florida has long been such a haven. Although its summer heat and humidity can be brutal, some people don't mind. Those who do object can arrange to spend that part of the year in a more temperate part of the county, usually by keeping one's residence up North. However, you will have to become a Florida resident if you plan to take advantage of the all the financial benefits that the state offers. Seven states have no income tax (others are Alaska, Nevada, South Dakota, Texas, Washington, and Wyoming), and not only is Florida on that list, but it also offers homestead protection that shields residents from losing their homes to a creditor or through any other lien but a mortgage. Although no retiree plans to file for bankruptcy, it is good to know that if the unthinkable should occur, you'll continue to have a roof over your head.

Other Florida tax advantages include a provision that the assessed value of a home cannot rise more than 3 percent in any given year.

That means that its market value will increase more than assessed value over time because of the untaxed increase.

In order to qualify for all the benefits, you must intend that your Florida residence is your primary one. The determination is made based on the totality of factors such as an officially recorded declaration of domicile, proof of Florida voter registration, a Florida driver's license, and evidence that you pay for utilities on your home there (bills and canceled checks will suffice).

To make sure that residents aren't cheating by spending too much time elsewhere, Florida insists that they spend a minimum of six months and one day in the state. If officials suspect you've not been living up to the letter of the law (and they monitor closely), you will be asked to offer such evidence as receipts for restaurants and other on-site activities and/or utility bills proving that your residence uses more electricity in months that require air conditioning or heating.

* * * * * *

Retiring Abroad

For romance and advance, what could be more glamorous or romantic than spending the rest of your life in a foreign country? Year-round strolls along the beach in Mexico or Belize . . . buying fresh croissants for your morning coffee at a *boulangerie* across the street from your Paris apartment . . . growing fresh herbs in the backyard of your Tuscany cottage . . . reveling in the art treasures of Amsterdam or Rome . . . the daydreams could go on and on.

The reality is a whole nother story, and one you should consider with far greater thought than relocating to another part of the United States.

Access to quality health care is a major factor for seniors. Although many countries can deliver medical services that are as good as and sometimes better than here, the care and cost can differ according to the type of treatment and by city or region. In many cases, you may prefer to come back to the US for certain procedures. Since Medicare coverage doesn't extend outside the US, you would have to look into private health insurance or, if in a country such as Mexico, buy into its national health plan.

Living abroad makes employment more complicated if you plan to continue or return to work. You would be competing against natives for even part-time positions, and being granted a work visa or permit could take a very long wait.

Taxes are an allied factor. The IRS taxes income no matter where American citizens live. Our laws also collect income tax from retirees who move their assets to a foreign country. And not every country has a treaty with the US that prevents double taxation. You'll want to discuss all the financial implications of a move with your accountant or financial planner who is expert in international matters.

The emotional aspects of living abroad will have an impact on your family. You'll be far away from your children, grandchildren, and other family members, and, as good as emailing and Skype-type videoing may be, you won't see them grow (or age) as you otherwise would. Moreover, their visiting you or your returning to America to see them can be costly and daunting.

Then, too, Americans living abroad can suffer from feelings of isolation, particularly when they aren't fluent in the local language or understand the subtleties of the local culture. The support system of an American or at least an international expatriate network in the area would be a source of essential information and, if and when you become homesick, familiar shoulders to lean on. You would also be grateful for emotional support in the event living abroad becomes overwhelming and you or your significant other starts in with, "Why did I let you drag me into this mess?"

As with relocating to other parts of the US, you'd want to spend several months in a prospective foreign area before making a commitment to a permanent move. As much time as you have spent there before, you would give yourself a different and more acute perspective of the country as well as the time to locate your ultimate residence and members of the American community that would help make retiring abroad a daydream come true.

5

DO UNTO OTHERS: OPPORTUNITIES TO VOLUNTEER

"As you grow older, you will discover that you have two hands, one for helping yourself and the other for helping others."

—Sam Levenson

Remember all those occasions when you were asked to give a piece of your time and energies to help an organization or a cause? "Gee, I'd really like to," you replied, "if only I had the time." Well, my friend, now you have the time. The question has become "How do you want to give away a part of yourself?"

If you need any further urging, let's start by enumerating the benefits of volunteering. It gets you out of your shell and connects you to others. One of the best ways of making new friends and strengthening existing friendships is a shared activity.

Such contact with others on a regular basis creates and maintains a solid social support system that is of immeasurable benefit, especially through challenging times. Moreover, volunteering enhances social skills and sense of self-esteem, important to people who may find themselves upset by aspects of retirement or aging.

Even if you can't easily leave your house because of limited mobility or family commitments, you can still do volunteer work via telephone or the Internet. To cite a few examples, you can use your literary or artistic skills to write or do graphic designing for newsletters of organizations whose aims you support, or do telephone solicitations for donations. Volunteer telephone "hotlines" need staff to do interventions in emotional and other medical emergencies and then offer support thereafter (you'll first be trained how to do it).

There are also less altruistic reasons for volunteering. For those who are thinking about returning to work, volunteering will facilitate the transition by getting you back to your former field or by trying a new one. For example, someone who is entertaining the idea of becoming a veterinarian's assistant can volunteer at an animal shelter where on-the-job training and gaining experience will increase one's marketability for a paying position there or elsewhere.

Whatever the motive, that volunteers make their communities a better place is indisputable. Indeed, they make the world a better place. Whether or not you believe in karma, volunteering makes you a better person too. In the words of Sir James Barrie, those who bring sunshine to the lives of others cannot keep it from themselves.

* * * * * *

Getting Started

Let's begin with another ask-yourself list.

- Would you like to get out or do volunteer work at home?
- How much time can you spend each week?
- How far would you travel from home?
- Would you want to confine yourself to helping one organization or spread your talents by helping several?
- Would you prefer to work with other people or by yourself?
- Would you rather interface with the people whom you're helping, or are you a behind-the-scenes type?

- Would you prefer to help children or adults? If children, which age range(s)?
- Would working with animals appeal to you?
- Are there political or religious/ethical reasons that would prevent your participating in certain activities? On the other hand, are there political or religious/ethical causes to which you are attracted?
- Have you skills such as writing, music, or athletics that you might want to use?
- Have you a professional background (e.g., business, medicine, law, or engineering) that you can use to mentor young people?
- Did you participate in volunteer efforts when you were younger, such as through religious groups or youth organizations as the Boy or Girl Scouts? Or did you volunteer while you were working through your business? If you did, are they the kinds of activities you might want to do again?

As with earlier self-tests in this book, there are no objectively correct answers, only correct-for-you ones that may suggest ways to donate your time and energies.

* * * * * *

How to Find Volunteering Opportunities

Start close to home. Do any of your friends, neighbors, or relatives do volunteer work? Does what they do sound appealing? Does the organization need additional help, and, if so, would volunteering there fit into your schedule?

If nothing comes from asking volunteers whom you know, look around your community. Is there a senior center? A hospital or hospice? A house of worship that has a soup kitchen or thrift shop? An animal shelter? Chances are good that any or all would be grateful for your services in some way.

Volunteering needn't be limited to existing opportunities. High schools, colleges, and professional schools hold reunions every five or ten years. Your class chairperson or committee will welcome your assistance with open alma mater arms. Do you look back nostalgically at summer camp years? If the camp is still in existence, get in touch with the owner about organizing a reunion.

If you're still stumped, here are areas that might strike your fancy:

Literacy

It's difficult for those of us who can read to imagine what life must be like for people whose literacy skills are lacking or indeed absent. That latter category doesn't apply only to newcomers from non-English-speaking countries; more native-born Americans who one would imagine have barely a rudimentary ability to read and write. That's why literacy programs are so necessary and so valuable.

Literacy programs offer a range of opportunities: basic reading and writing skills (basic arithmetic skills too) for adults; English as a second language (abbreviated ESL) for immigrants and others who grew up in households where only a foreign language was spoken; and college preparation where high school students are assisted in applying to schools, filling out financial aid forms, and preparing for college entrance exams.

Just because you can read and write doesn't mean you can step right into the role of tutor. Although prerequisites vary according to the organization, most require volunteers to be at least eighteen years of age with a high school or equivalent degree, and—no surprise here—the ability to read and write English fluently. Teaching experience is usually not a requirement, because most organizations have their tutors first take part in training workshops and sometimes annual refresher courses. Organizations will also require a commitment of a minimum number of hours per week.

Literacy organizations allow flexibility about when tutors meet with students: mornings, afternoons, early evenings, and weekends.

Most sessions take place at the organization's headquarters, if there is one, or else a library, a school, or a house of worship.

The training program often includes sensitivity training, because tutors need to display patience when working with students from other countries and cultural backgrounds and with students who will have a range of learning capacities and speeds. English grammar, spelling, and pronunciation are far more idiosyncratic than most native English speakers realize, and you'll be taught how to help students overcome any embarrassment or frustration that accompanies their learning curves. You'll also find out how to prepare lesson plans, select and use approved workbooks, and develop techniques for presenting vocabulary and grammar, as well as basic writing skills.

Libraries, public and private schools, and senior centers know about literacy programs in your area. Even handier are these two websites where you can type in your zip code and then be informed about the nearest opportunities:

http://www.proliteracy.org/find-a-program.
https://literacydirectory.org/?op=ld&mode=volunteers.

* * * * * *

Foster Grandparents and Senior Companions

Although some retirees may welcome a freedom that includes little to no responsibilities to children and grandchildren, others look back with nostalgia at their parenting era and regret the "empty nest" syndrome. Such people will be interested in the Foster Grandparents program. These volunteers aged fifty-five and older serve as role models, mentors, and friends to children with special needs. Assignments include one-on-one tutoring, and counseling and emotional support for abused or neglected children, troubled teenagers, and young mothers. Programs take place in schools, hospitals, juvenile correctional institutions, daycare facilities, and Head Start centers. Volunteers receive preservice orientation and training from the organization, and supplemental accidental and liability insurance where they will serve. Those at certain income levels also receive a small stipend.

For further information, see www. nationalservice.gov/programs/senior-corps/foster-grandparents.

If working with youngsters isn't in your future, look into becoming a Senior Companion. You will give assistance and friendship to two to four adults who live independently at home but who have difficulty with daily living tasks like shopping and paying bills. In addition, companions become available to give families or professional caregivers valuable time off from their duties.

Like the Foster Grandparents program, Senior Companions is under the auspices of the Corporation for National & Community Service. See www.nationalservice.gov/programs/senior-corps/senior-companions.

* * * * * *

Animal Shelters

A few years ago, an elderly, childless widow mourned the passing of her beloved cat, one of the few remaining links with her late husband. The loss was made even more depressing because at her age, adopting another cat might mean that the animal would survive her with an uncertain future, or she might have to move to an assisted living facility that prohibited pets.

An acquaintance had a brainstorm. She had heard about a Pennsylvania animal rescue shelter where youngsters practice their reading skills by reading to kittens and cats. The kids improve their proficiency while the felines cozy up to or sit in their laps and thus become better socialized. The woman's acquaintance pointed out that an animal rescue shelter was within walking distance of the widow's house. Why didn't she see whether she could read to the children and animals? Not that the woman, a voracious reader, needed any practice with that skill, but she'd mingle with an appreciative furry audience that would benefit from human contact. It was worth a try.

Normally shy about such matters, the woman summoned up the courage to approach the shelter's director. The director agreed to see how well the idea would work, and a week or two later was delighted to see that cats, kittens, and older, non-boisterous dogs were giving as much attention and affection to the woman as they received from her.

As this anecdote shows, animal shelters benefit from a variety of assistance. Whether it's socializing kittens and cats, taking dogs for walks, or assisting with office procedures, publicity campaigns, and fundraising solicitations and events, you can enhance the quality of the animals' lives—and your own. Talk about warm fuzzy feelings!

Phone or stop in at a shelter in your area to see what's available. Finding one is no more difficult than consulting the phone book or asking at a veterinarian's office or a pet shop. And here's a website: http://theshelter-petproject.org/shelters. Enter your ZIP code and click "search."

If you have the time, space, and patience, you might volunteer to raise a puppy to become a guide dog for the blind [https://www.guidingeyes.org/volunteer/puppy-raising/] or a companion to assist people with physical limitations [http://www.cci.org/]. Although relinquishing the dog you've raised can be heart-wrenching (or so several people have admitted), the knowledge that the animal will improve the quality of its new owner's life is worth the effort. And besides, there is always a new puppy waiting to be raised.

* * * * * *

Conservation

Hunting, fishing, hiking, canoeing and rafting, mountain biking, bird-watching, observing wildflower and foliage scenery, nature photography—anyone who takes advantage of our country's natural resources is aware how the quality of outdoor life is threatened by climate change and pollution from human, industrial, and agricultural waste. If you're such a participant or spectator, you have a vested interest in helping conservation organizations and agencies maintain and restore our environmental heritage.

In addition to well-known national organizations like the National Audubon Society [www.audubon.org], Sierra Club [www.sierraclub.org], Trout Unlimited [www.tu.org], and the Wilderness Society [wilderness.org], the federal US Fish and Wildlife Service offers many opportunities for volunteer participation [www.fws.gov/volunteers/index.html]. Activities include banding birds at wildlife refuges, raising fish at hatcheries, restoring habitats, conducting wildlife surveys, leading tours, and lecturing at agency sites and at schools. On-the-job training is provided where required. Volunteer opportunities are available at more than five hundred refuges and hatcheries throughout the United States. This state-by-state list will help you find one near you: www.fws.gov/volunteers/volProgramList.html.

Other Outdoors Organizations

American Rivers protects and restores waterways: www.americanrivers.org/take-action/cleanup/volunteer/.

The Environmental Protection Agency's Adopt Your Watershed focuses on preserving and maintaining healthy local watersheds: water.epa.gov/action/adopt/index.cfm.

The National Parks Service offers volunteer opportunities in its four hundred parks: www.nps.gov/getinvolved/volunteer.htm. Another website shows the range of outdoors activities: www.volunteer.gov.

* * * * * *

Business Mentoring

Many retired executives who want to keep their hand in the world of commerce as well as lend a hand to new and established small businesses volunteer their time and expertise through SCORE, the organization formerly known as the "Service Corps of Retired Executives" but now calling itself "Counselors to America's Small Business." SCORE offers face-to-face mentoring sessions and also presents business workshops and seminars for a fee. In addition, "Ask SCORE" offers online counseling.

Mentoring services include developing business plans like promotion, publicity, advertising, and other marketing strategies. Financial planning includes long- and short-term borrowing, balance sheets, and cash flow charts. Where appropriate, discussions would involve manufacturing strategies both domestically and importing from abroad. The value of such assistance comes from mentors' experiences of having "been there and done that"—clients profit from mentors' successes and mistakes.

In SCORE, no mentor can be paid for any advice or other service, in order to protect clients from anyone who might become an advisor to get business leads. Clients who want to hire their mentors must wait until the guru resigns as a SCORE volunteer.

For details on becoming a mentor or becoming a client if you're thinking about starting a new business, go to www.score.org.

Another matchup organization is MicroMentor, whose website asks specific questions about your entrepreneurial ambitions and then introduces you to what it considers to be your most suitable advisor: www.micromentor.org.

* * * * * *

Protecting the Interests of Children at Risk

CASA, or Court Appointed Special Advocates, is a network of 951 community-based programs that recruit, train, and support adults to provide support for the best interests of abused and neglected children in courtrooms and communities. Volunteer advocates, who are court-appointed, investigate each child's history and situation in order to present the court with critical information with regard to the child's rights and needs while in foster care. Volunteers remain on the case until the child is placed in suitable permanent homes. For information: www.casaforchildren.org/.

* * * * * *

Riding for the Handicapped

You don't have to know which end of the horse gets the carrot to become a part of an equine therapy program for physically and emotionally challenged youngsters and adults with such challenges as muscular dystrophy, autism, multiple sclerosis, and bipolar disorder. This program is more commonly known as Riding for the Handicapped.

All that's required is a willingness to help such people expand their capabilities through mounted exercises. Activities take place at public and private riding stables in urban as well as suburban and rural locations. Volunteers typically serve as side-walkers, walking on each side of the horse to help keep the rider in the saddle while someone else leads the animal and the therapist works with the rider on specific exercises. Anyone who has volunteered or even just witnessed a session will appreciate the physical and emotional benefits and feel the rider's joy of accomplishment.

For further information about a program near you, inquire at nearby riding stables (if the barn doesn't host a program, someone there will know one that does) or a tack shop, or see www.narah.org.

* * * * * *

Museum, Zoo, Aquarium, or Public Gardens Docent

A docent (from the Latin "to teach" and pronounced "DOE-cent") is a lecturer-guide at a museum, zoo, aquarium, or public garden who leads tours and explains the background and significance of the artwork, flora, or fauna on display. It is usually done on a voluntary basis and according to the docent's schedule. An interest, if not a background, in art history, science (if it's a natural history or science museum), animals or fish (if a zoo or aquarium), or botany (if a public garden) is extremely helpful, although not always essential. What is indispensable is an outgoing personality that includes an ability to engage an audience and the knack of asking and answering questions.

Once you decide on a facility, take a docent-led tour to see what the job entails. If becoming a guide still appeals to you, ask the docent or someone at the front desk about where to apply. If you're not up on the institution's permanent collections (including all species if a zoo, aquarium, or garden) and any upcoming special exhibits, you'll want to do your homework in advance of your interview with the docent program's administrator. Applicants who have been accepted undergo a training program, after which they are customarily observed as they lead their first few tours.

To see what's available, contact the museum, zoo, aquarium, or public gardens of your choice:

- Accredited museums: www.aam-us.org/docs/accreditation/list-of-accredited-museums.pdf?sfvrsn=0.
- Accredited zoos and aquariums: www.aza.org/current-accreditation-list/.
- Public gardens: www.garden.org/public_gardens/.

* * * * * *

Creating a Family History

"Grandpa, did you ever know your grandpa?" That question from his young grandson galvanized Grandpa into action. After setting his grandson down for a tale of family history, he decided to create a more permanent record. Interviewing his only surviving aunt as well as his cousins, he sketched a family tree that he filled in with reminiscences by his author and cousins before repeating the process with his wife's side of the family.

Turning the project into a true family affair, Grandpa enlisted the services of his grandson and an older granddaughter. They videotaped the interviews and supplied questions that never would have occurred to him, such as "Which was the first movie you ever saw?" and "Who was the most famous person you ever met or saw?" The answers sent the kids to their computers where they downloaded and organized appropriate photos and maps. The result was a family history DVD that contained narration, video excerpts, and illustrations. And, thanks to the ease of desktop publishing, the text and illustrations became an accompanying paperback book.

When Grandpa couldn't help brag about the project, listeners requested his expert assistance in trying their hand at similar chronicles. One person focused on an uncle who returned from World War II a victim of life-altering, post-traumatic stress disorder (a term not formally in use at the time). Another went back far enough to find an ancestor who settled the family's hometown.

Now what, you may be asking yourself, has this to do with volunteering? Simply this: Grandpa began to spend time at a senior citizen center interviewing and taping residents, with their stories then given to the residents' friends and relatives. In fact, the project became so popular that the center considered starting a personal history group where residents would swap tales of their youth.

From the mouths of babes . . .

* * * * * *

On a much less formal level, anyone who sings and/or plays an instrument can perform as a solo act or as a band with other musician friends at a variety of venues: soup kitchens, fund-raising parties, lunches and dinners, senior centers, retirement homes, and hospitals. You needn't be a concert-caliber musician to qualify; your audiences will be delighted for the diversion. Audience sing-alongs of familiar songs like "You Are My Sunshine" and "She'll Be Coming 'Round the Mountain" or carols during Christmas season are always popular and a beneficial way to raise the audience's spirits. Nursing home staff members marvel at how patients who rarely if ever spoke came out of their shells at the sound of songs they knew.

Get in touch with the administrator or director of the venue of your choice to set a date.

* * * * * *

If you still haven't come up with an area of interest and an organization to make use of your services, several choose-your-own-activities websites will lend you a hand. Type in the kind of volunteer work you might like to do and your address or just your ZIP code, and let the algorithms work their magic:

- Volunteers of America: www.voa.org.
- Volunteer Match: www.volunteermatch.org.
- Volunteer Resource Center: www.idealist.org.
- Points of Light: www.pointsoflight.org.
- Create the Good: www.createthegood.org.

* * * * * *

No matter which organization you approach, you should make certain that you and the group are a good fit. During your initial and any subsequent interviews, take a proactive approach and ask as many questions as you're asked. You'll want to know about the exact kind of work, time commitments, the location, the person or group to whom you'll report, and the amount and type of training involved.

By the same token, don't be reluctant to speak up if, once your assignment has begun in the event, it doesn't meet with your expectations. Talk to your supervisor or the volunteer program coordinator about why your involvement isn't working out to your expectations. It may well be that you're being asked to spend more time than you can afford to or you were moved to an inconvenient location. Perhaps you dislike your colleagues or you find yourself doing assignments you hadn't been told about when you took on the job. Rather than resign, first see whether accommodations can be made to the satisfaction of both you and the program.

If not, however, you may be obliged to find another opportunity that will make you happier, but in no event should you give up on volunteering. As Winston Churchill said, "We make a living by what we get, but we make a life by what we give."

6

TRAVEL

"The real voyage of discovery consists not in seeking new landscapes, but in having new eyes."

—Marcel Proust

People in the workplace typically describe vacations as two or three weeks away from the slave mines, or more time if you're self-employed and can afford it (teachers and other academics are a special case). But now that you're retired, and especially if your spouse or significant other is too, holidays acquire a new dimension. With no real or metaphorical calendar on which to check off days and no time clock to punch, your freedom to roam the earth is limited only by physical or medical restrictions, family commitments, and your imagination and your bank account.

Two retired and well-traveled friends generously offered their advice. The first is a former schoolteacher whose husband is also retired. Sometimes on her own, sometimes as a couple, she pursues a wide range of cultural and musical interests. Here's what she had to say:

"At age fifty-five-plus you don't need more souvenirs to clutter the basement, so cruise ships that feature shopping sprees at ports of call wouldn't be for you. We're partial to Road Scholar (formerly known as Elderhostel) education tours for more than just a superficial travel experience. In addition to biking in Moab, Utah, we've taken urban tours of Minneapolis, Austin, Portland (Oregon), and Lafayette (Louisiana), and through France's Provence region where Van Gogh and Cezanne lived and worked.

"Local teachers, artists and art critics, film critics, and music experts are guest lecturers. Attendees tend to be receptive to learning, considerate of others with regard to scheduling, and they're there to learn. The only drawbacks we've encountered are having to rely on public transportation in large cities, and accommodations that can be average in comfort and often far away from city centers.

"Smithsonian Journeys feature tours with extra comfort and superb lectures that focus on very specific programs such as art and architecture in Pittsburgh where we visited Frank Lloyd Wright's Fall-

ingwater building. We also enjoyed the range of opera, theater, dance, and classical and popular music at the Speleto Festival Charleston, South Carolina.

"Tauck Tours also combine education with service and luxury, with little touches that make the difference. When we finished seeing the sobering horrors of Auschwitz in Poland, the tour director had restorative glasses of schnapps waiting for us back at the bus. On a trip in France that included Normandy, Brittany, and the Loire Valley, our last stop was Paris. We stayed at the Hotel Lutetia, infamous in World War II German Occupation history and noted for its art deco style. On our beds the last night were "Jazz at the Lutetia" CDs, another very thoughtful gesture.

"Traveco Tours of Africa, South America, and the Galapagos are small and sumptuous, with an emphasis on eating and drinking that can prove overwhelming for senior stomachs.

"We've taken cruises too. Land trips give more of a sense of place than cruises do, but cruises offer the convenience of having to unpack and repack only once. Something that older travelers would want to take into consideration is that living out of a suitcase can become tiresome on lengthy tours that change hotels every day or two."

* * * * * *

This advice comes from a labor mediator whose work affords time to travel with her husband, an international businessman. They enjoy vacationing in the company of her husband's brother and his wife, but since the brother has mobility issues, the four of them find that taking cruises is the most satisfactory way to be together.

"I can speak only for Princess Cruises since that's what we've taken, but I've been extremely impressed. There are many handicap-accessible stateroom options on the ship. Elevators and gently sloped ramps exist wherever a change of deck or level is required. All theaters and lounge areas that are 'stepped' also have a reserved wheelchair-accessible area that is easy to get to and has a good view of the action.

"The staff is trained in dealing with wheelchairs and walkers at dinner, and people were seated with no trouble at a variety of tables and dining options. The upper deck's twenty-four-hour buffet was accessible, but might have been a bit of a challenge for getting around from stage to stage. I think that's a trivial issue.

"As for on-shore excursions, nearly all the buses that were commissioned by the company in the various ports of call had a rear entrance with an elevator ramp for wheelchair travelers or anyone with limited stair-climbing ability. The cruise line is also pretty good at noting which tours are not appropriate for limited-mobility people (the classical Greek ruins in the Turkish town of Ephesus was a good example—it was tough even for the young and athletic because of the footing).

"The rating systems are not foolproof, however. The tour of Italy's Florence began with a lovely bus ride from the port through the countryside followed by a brief walk from the bus to the first 'sight' in the town square near the Pitti Palace. Again, the walking wasn't terribly strenuous, and the footing was pretty good. Nevertheless, there was a one-hour wait to get into the Uffizi Gallery. Standing all that time was tough on my brother-in-law, and not all that great for the rest of us either. The same thing happened in Rome. The bus parked in an underground parking garage about a half-mile uphill walk to the Piazza San Marco. The tour was advertised as limited-mobility-friendly, but it definitely wasn't. One poor lady who used a walker nearly became lost because she couldn't keep up with the others in our group.

"This was in stark contrast to the Hawaii cruise on which we had several wheelchair-bound passengers. Most of the land tours labeled as handicap-accessible truly were (partly a function of still being in the United States, I suspect). There were even three tours in which the passengers had to be shuttled by boat from the ship to the shore, and with one exception, those, too, were handicap accessible (with tethering for the wheelchair, as I remember).

"On a less chipper note, it is also a good idea to check directly with the cruise line to learn about onboard hospital facilities. Princess is quite good on that score. At least one MD is available for appointments or is 'on call' around the clock, and there's an infirmary staffed with physician assistants and nurses, as well as a basic dispensing pharmacy. The facility itself can handle most emergencies, such as cuts, broken bones, and even cardio-aversion (shocking a heart back into rhythm). In case of a serious problem, the captain will take the ship to the nearest port in order to transport the ailing passenger to a reliable hospital. This happened on a cruise we took on the way to Puerto Vallarta, and I was truly impressed by how the captain handled the announcement to the passengers, and how the passengers reacted with sympathy rather than sulking. (In that regard, you might want to investigate travel insurance for just such a medical contingency.) It is my understanding that cruise ships must meet some international standard of available health facilities, but I suspect the level and quality of those facilities will vary widely. There should be a person you can contact directly (as Princess has) to discuss particular health concerns before you reserve your trip.

"For overseas travel that is not entirely on a cruise line, it's not a bad idea to discuss with your physician what precautions you should take. For example, with my husband's frequent trips to London, we were given recommendations for good cardiology specialists there who could be called upon in a crisis, as well as suggestions about which hospitals are better than others in that specialty. If you have a breathing apparatus, you should make sure you'll have available oxygen refills if needed. For CPAP machines, you should have several foreign electric plug adapters. You can also ask any foreign hotel of any repute for an extension cord if the plug is in an inconvenient place in relation to the bed.

"We have also made a practice of carrying an adequate supply of prescription medication for the entire trip in at least two separate places. That means a double supply—in my case, my computer bag and my handbag. My husband carries his in his pocket and his carry-on. I also have a medic-alert bracelet, since I have an allergy to some medications.

"Based on my observations, cruises are a wonderful way to see new and different places even when your mobility is limited. The mobility-challenged people we have seen on our cruises varied from travelers with multiple sclerosis and cerebral palsy in their early thirties to at least mid-eighties and perhaps older still.

"Even though some people can't or don't choose to disembark at every port, a cruise ship is a floating resort, and an elegant one at that, with spas, pools, and entertainment. Also, to prepare travelers for every stop on Princess Cruises is an education film on that particular location offered either in a theater setting or broadcast into your stateroom or both. In addition, a library offers a huge selection of books that go far beyond paperback novel 'beach reads,' and usually a variety of puzzles, Sudoku, and board games to borrow.

"And if I may add a final thought about any mode of travel or accommodation: if you have limited mobility issues, such as requiring a cane, walker, or wheelchair, try to get more specific information than simply a facility's assertion that it's a 'handicap-friendly' site. Take it from someone who knows. After a week in a wheelchair following knee surgery, I found that handicap-accessible places often were not. The 'accessible' ramp at the Cornell International Labor Relations School was built over a section of the steps to the building. The ramp was at a 30-degree angle up to a door that opened out beyond the ramp. Oh, and did I mention it was under the ice floe of the roofline? In my case it was merely annoying, and I had assistance. But I would not in any way call it 'accessible.' Being caught in such situations can take all the pleasure out of a vacation."

Other people offered other thoughts on the subject of cruises:

There's a wide panorama of special-interest cruises. If music is your bag, look for ones that focus on your favorite genre such as classical, jazz, bluegrass, or country music. With musicians and groups/bands on-board for daily concerts, you often have the chance to join in on informal jam sessions or the classical equivalent if you play an instrument. Other cruises sail to ports of call known for art, archeology, and literature, or the cuisine and beverages of specific regions of the world. Or if you're looking in the social sense, cruises exist for singles of all gender preferences. Simply entering your interest + "cruises" into a computer search engine will reveal the attractions, places of embarkation, destinations, duration, and cost.

Although travelers who are susceptible to severe motion sickness may think they're not cruise material, you can still enjoy a sea voyage with a bit of planning. Choose a large ship on which you're less likely feel its motion than you would on a smaller and lighter vessel. Book a stateroom at the center of the ship on a lower deck, the most stable location. Select an itinerary that frequently stops in port rather than one that involves many consecutive days at sea. Be sure to pack over-the-counter motion-sickness medications like Dramamine, natural remedies like ginger tablets, and motion-sickness wristbands (the ship's medical personnel, who are accustomed to dealing with this problem, will have ample supplies of replacement items).

Cruises have long been noted for their plentiful round-the-clock food offerings. Toward that end, many lines enlist the services of well-known chefs to design imaginative gourmet menus. However, anyone who is a picky eater or on strict diets should determine in advance whether the ship offers suitable options for anyone who adheres to a vegetarian, vegan, gluten-free, kosher, or halal diet.

* * * * * *

Travel with The Entire Family

Cruises are a good way for your entire multigenerational family to take a vacation together, the ship providing a setting in which you, your children, and grandchildren can spend time getting to know each other better. And when you or they have had enough "togetherness" time, everyone can go off and find activities on his or her own, from organized sports and games to stretching out on a deck chair and staring at the horizon until you doze off.

Another popular option is a dude ranch. Even if your dreams of becoming the next Roy Rogers or Dale Evans have faded into the sunset, you and your family can enjoy sedate trail rides on wellmannered steeds through beautiful scenery. And while ranch hands teach your grandkids to throw a lasso or ride a mechanical bull, the older generations can fish in the ranch's pond or stream, drive into town for shopping, explore scenic areas, or just sit in a comfortable chair on the porch or under a shade tree while knitting or reading a good book.

Yet other popular family vacation choices are Disney World and Disneyland. If you've never been there, seeing it through a child's eyes makes the place even more magical, while adult eyes will marvel at its technology and logistics.

Please take notice that if you're traveling with people who are much younger than you, bear in mind that they have the energy you no longer have. A pal and his wife who took their children to Paris as high school graduation gifts decades earlier repeated the gift for their granddaughters. Their week in the City of Lights was again memorable for the sights, but now my friend discovered that he didn't have the vigor for a full day of walking that he had a generation ago. That plus a blister from breaking in a pair of shoes he bought for the trip combined, as he put it, to feeling at day's end as if he had been on Napoleon's retreat from Moscow.

* * * * * *

For further information:

- Road Scholars: roadscholar.org.
- Smithsonian Journeys: smithsonianjourneys.org.

- Tauck Tours: tauck.com.
- Traveco: travcotravel.com.
- Cruise Critic (special-interest cruises): www.cruisecritic.com.
- Dude Ranchers Association: duderanch.org.
- Disney World: disneyworld.disney.go.com.

7

ENCORE EMPLOYMENT, OR RETURNING TO WORK

"Even if you fall on your face, you're still moving forward."
—Victor Kiam

Throughout your working life, you daydreamed about retirement. When the blessed day finally came, you rejoiced at the prospect of freedom from early-morning alarm clock awakenings, boring staff meetings, production quotas, and other less-than-rosy aspects of your 9-to-5 life.

But somewhere down the road, you discovered that your nest egg didn't work out the way you had planned. Or that divorce, your spouse's death, an adult child who needs your financial support, or another lifestyle change radically altered your financial needs. Or else you came up with a brilliant idea or stumbled across a struggling company that you're sure you can turn around into a successful venture. Or—and, yes, it can happen—you realize that you like working. Volunteering isn't sufficient—you seek both the emotional fulfillment and the financial compensation.

Whether by choice or necessity, you're not alone. Between the years 2006 and 2011 the number of employed Americans decreased on every age-group level except for those who were fifty-five and older. According to the Department of Labor, this group accounted for an increase of over four million jobs. Among the reasons is that employers have found that seniors between sixty and seventy-four are demonstrably more productive in many ways than their younger counterparts are (one boss fumes whenever he comes across staff members glued to social media on cell phones or computers while on company time). Then, too, older employees tend to remain at the same job three times longer than younger ones do (a survey showed that sixty-five-plus-year-old workers stayed in their second jobs for almost ten years on average); plus they have a better punctuality record. They can also provide an older, more mature image that well-established, conservative companies want to project.

And that's more than just wishful thinking. As Barbara Strauch writes in her book *The Secret Life of the Grown-Up Brain,* scientific research indicates that middle-aged intelligence improves in important organizational functions and even contributes to a more optimistic outlook on life than its younger counterpart. It recognizes patterns faster, makes sounder judgments, and comes up with innovative solutions to problems. Sure, you may momentarily forget what you did with the house keys or where you left your car in the mall parking lot, but, in balance, your brain remains very much a marketable asset.

That's not to say that employers are hanging out the window looking for seniors who are eager to get back in harness. There are several reasons. Applicants who have been out of specific lines of work, especially in the technical world, lack the most up-to-date skills, especially those who have been out of the workforce for several years. Whether the applicant is worth training is a judgment call that bosses may or may not care to make. Some companies strive for a "youthful" image that graying hair and un-hip clothing don't convey. With regard to corporate finances, insuring an older employee may cost the company more than someone half the person's age.

* * * * * *

Finances

Rather than blindly dive back into the employment pool, take time to examine the financial consequences as you decide what you want to do, where you want to do it, and for how many days a week. For example, although returning to work will generate income, there will be the expense of getting to and from the job. If you'll drive, you'll buy gas on a regular basis, perhaps pay tolls and parking, and incur wear-and-tear on your vehicle. You may be obliged to look the part, so good-bye to seven-day-a-week floppies, T-shirts, and jeans or shorts, and hello to a closetful of suitable office attire. Then, too, you may have to factor in the outlay for childcare if you have young dependents or, more likely, dayworkers or fulltime caregivers to assist older relatives you've been looking after.

Your income from other sources may be diminished. Whether Social Security income is reduced depends on your age. For example, the Social Security Administration mandates normal retirement age as between sixty-six and sixty-seven for people born in 1943 or later. If you're younger, $1 in benefits will be deducted for every $2 you earn above the annual limit ($15,480 in 2014). Also, benefits may become taxable when you exceed a certain amount of salary. The good news is that as soon as you reach your normal retirement age, benefits are no longer reduced, despite how much you earn.

Many people under the age of sixty-five who might otherwise retire or enter the freelance world continue to work solely because of health insurance. If you're sixty-five or older and now covered by Medicare, be sure to check with a prospective employer to see how their insurance coverage would affect your Medicare. Or, if you have private health insurance, find out how your benefits and coverage compare. There may be reasons to stay with the coverage you now have. The same argument applies to pension plans and 401(k)s.

Even working part-time or freelancing will have a financial impact. All things considered, advice from your accountant and/or investment counselor is well worth seeking.

* * * * * *

Where to Look

Many if not most retirees going back to work start by looking in their former profession or industry. That's a natural response: you know the ins and outs of the business, and you're likely still to know people you can use as contacts if not prospective employers. That's all well and good if you liked the profession or industry. On the other hand, if you left with a sour taste along the lines of "that business has changed for the worst—I don't understand it anymore," you'll scour the highways for something you like better. That might be a field in which you did volunteer work where, although you can no longer afford not to be paid, you now have a marketable amount of expertise. Or it can be an entirely new area that you wouldn't mind learning. A lawyer who

hadn't practiced in decades after going into the family retail business had kept his law license caught up on the intricacies of elder law and now enjoys a thriving clientele. "It's a growth industry," he pointed out with considerable pleasure and accuracy.

Three other fields that require specialized training, but can be well worth the time and expense, are nurse-practitioner or physician's assistant, paralegal, and real estate broker. Many older patients and clients find an equally mature person more sympathetic and reassuring to deal with, especially when the professional or paraprofessional has been through similar experiences.

You might also consider consultancies and/or research work in areas in which you have expertise. Or telephone sales, fund-raising solicitation, customer service, and help-lines. Sales help at department stores or specialty shops are yet another good place to look.

When the actual searching begins, back-to-workers cite success from networking to find out about jobs that aren't advertised or by providing their information to employment agencies. Employers inquire inside and outside their companies for personnel suggestions. Tell everyone you know professionally and personally that you're actively seeking. You never know who knows of a promising lead or can think of someone else who might. Networking should be throwing not one but a handful of pebbles in a pond. The ripples from each conversation will widen and will also intersect: the more that people hear from a variety of sources about you, your interests, and your qualifications, the more likely you'll be to hear back with leads.

By the same token, cyber-networking via Facebook, LinkedIn (which is specifically intended for building professional networks), and other social media is another essential. Any retiree who thinks that social media are for only youngsters is wrong. They're for everyone. Facebook Friends have friends, and LinkedIn members are parts of chains. If you're not yet computer- or smartphone-savvy, your children or grandchildren can teach you.

You might also consider registering at temporary employment agencies even if you're contemplating a full-time job. In addition to earning money, becoming a temp or a part-time worker gets you back out into the marketplace, a useful psychological as well as physical wake-up transition, especially if you've been retired for some time. Many ex-retirees who did so found they enjoyed the kind of secretarial, administrative, or other work as well as the company where they toiled. The company liked them, and presto—full-time jobs.

Finding a new job may take a long time, but perseverance will pay off. An ex-retiree who spent more than a year looking before she was hired phrased her advice in financial terms: "Don't become discouraged or depressed—you can't afford to."

* * * * * *

Websites of Interest

- RetiredBrains [retiredbrains.com]: a broad source of information for seniors and retired people.
- Workforce50 [Workforce50.com]: for job-seeker age fifty and older (the site was formerly known as the Senior Job Bank).
- Seniors4Hire [seniors4hire.com]: also for job-seekers fifty and above.
- Jobs 4.0 [jobs4point0.com]: for job-seekers over the age of forty.
- Your Encore [yourencore.com]: for retired executives who want consulting and other positions with corporations.
- JobHunt [job-hunt.org]: links to websites of interest to retired job-seekers.

Two federal agencies may be of interest:

- USAJobs [help.usajobs.gov]: for federal job-seekers looking for employment at government agencies.

- The Small Business Administration [www.sba.gov/category/navigation-structure/starting-managing-business/starting-business] offers free counseling and instruction for anyone who wants to begin his or her own business.

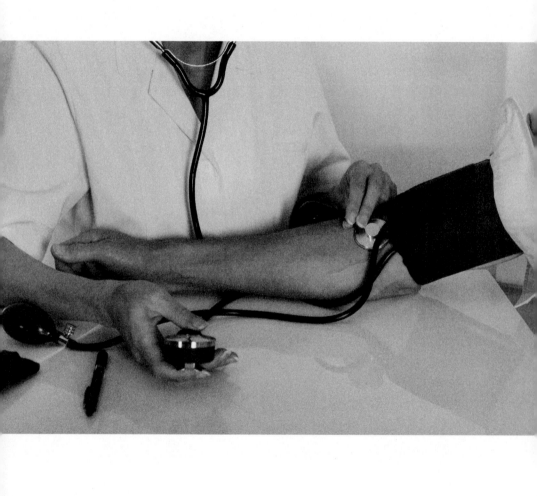

8

PLANNING FOR A HEALTHY RETIREMENT
by Laurence Burd, MD

"There's nothing more important than our good health—
that's our principal capital asset."
—Senator Arlen Specter

The most important factor to achieve your plans and dreams for retirement is your health. Any health professional will list eight essential
things to do to preserve your health during your later years (although
the advice holds true for any age): eat a well-balanced diet; maintain
the appropriate weight for your height; participate in a regular exercise program; avoid harmful habits like smoking and alcohol and drug
abuse; stay mentally active and be engaged with friends and family;
and participate in sports, hobbies, and/or part-time work that you really enjoy. Most importantly, be monitored on a regular basis by a
health care professional.

While these activities will help you achieve your retirement goals,
they cannot prevent the progress of aging that we all must experience
and deal with during midlife and beyond. An understanding of aging—
why it occurs and its symptoms and physical, mental, and emotional

effects—will help us realize why a good plan for maintaining health may delay the setbacks that occur during our retirement years.

At the outset, you may be interested to know that health is one of the most important considerations in making the decision to retire. "Growing Older in America: The Health and Retirement Study," conducted by the National Institute of Aging (NIA) in cooperation with the University of Michigan, followed more than twenty thousand men and women over fifty. The study found that 35 percent of people over fifty cited health as the most important reason to retire, an even stronger influence than financial considerations.

* * * * * *

Simply defined, aging is what happens to your body over time. Changes that occur are the result of decreases in the rate of cell growth and replication, glandular or hormonal secretion, slower utilization of foods and energy production (metabolism), and a decrease in the efficiency of your immune system that defends against infections and disease. Aging affects strength, agility, memory, and resistance. The rate at which we age is fairly constant, but that rate can be influenced by genetics, lifestyle, and disease.

As we age, our metabolism, the process that uses food to make energy, slows down due to a decrease in muscle mass and an increase in total body fat. These changes are due primarily to decreased exercise time, and, as we lose muscle mass, the problem perpetuates. Since muscle is more metabolic than fat, the number of calories you burn decreases. Hormones influence this relationship as well. Women who have gone through menopause tend to accumulate more fat in their buttocks and thighs and, similar to men, also experience an increase abdominal fat. These changes can cause a predisposition to cardiovascular disease, obesity, and diabetes. Because of this change in metabolism and an age-related development of resistance to insulin, the hormone that causes our cells to absorb the most common form of sugar—glucose for energy production—we become more predisposed to develop diabetes with all of its complications. Diabetes in turn can lead to heart, kidney, and eye disease.

* * * * * *

Decline of Organ Performance and Function

A decrease in the function of several organ systems begins long before the age of retirement and—please note—is accelerated by a sedentary lifestyle. By age twenty a lessening in the ability of the chest wall to stretch and a reduction in the number of air sacs in our lungs occur. In each succeeding decade the maximum amount of oxygen we can hold decreases by approximately 9 percent for men and 5 percent for women.

Gradual changes in your cardiovascular system occur as well. By age sixty-five there is a 20 percent to 30 percent decrease in the amount of blood that hearts can pump out each minute. Blood also undergoes a loss in ability to carry oxygen. Early adulthood blood pressure averages 120/80 millimeters of mercury. Aging causes blood vessel elasticity loss that results in a 10- to 40-millimeter of mercury increase in systolic (upper, higher reading) and diastolic (lower reading). Maximal heart rate decreases by about 10 beats per decade, although your resting heart rate does not change. Fat deposits form in arteries of the heart and other organs to limit blood flow and may cause disease.

Strength, a reflection of muscular system integrity, increases into our third decade and then levels off through our fifties and sixties. By the age of seventy it has fallen by 30 percent. By that age, your muscle mass has decreased by 40 percent, with the lower body more affected than the upper.

By age thirty-five, bone mass begins to decline by 1 percent per year; for women this increases to 2 percent after menopause. Joints begin to degenerate as a result of decreased elasticity of their connective tissue and of lubricating fluid, with the spine affected most prominently. Within your neurological system is a 15 percent reduction in nerve conduction accompanied by a concomitant decrease in neurons and brain mass. Total cholesterol increases with a decrease in HDL (the good type) cholesterol. Finally, normal aging brings a gradual loss of thirst, eyesight, taste, balance, and hearing.

* * * * * *

Common Complaints of the Retiree

The retirement years are a time of reflection, including thinking about physical, mental, and emotional changes. Invariably, you will begin to notice how your appearance is changing and how your body feels. Here are the most common aging complaints, the reasons they occur, and steps that you can take to avoid or modify these changes.

Wrinkles and Dry Skin

As the years progress, your skin experiences generalized thinning and loss of elasticity, and its ability to retain moisture is reduced. This combination of lack of moisture and loss of collagen and elastin makes the skin more prone to dryness, and your skin will start to sag, especially in the areas exposed to light that include the face, neck, and hands.

Preventing wrinkles involves using an effective lubricant long before wrinkles appear. Avoid spending too much time in the sun, smoking, exposure to central heating and air conditioning systems, sedentary lifestyle, environmental pollutants, traffic fumes, and drinking too much alcohol, all of which result in drying. Include in your diet essential nutrients and vitamins, particularly omega-3 essential fatty acids. Postmenopausal women might use creams and lotions that contain estrogen-like substances, although prolonged use of estrogen is not recommended and should be done only after consulting a physician.

Dry skin more often occurs on lower legs, elbows, and forearms. The skin feels scaly and rough and is often accompanied by an intense itchiness. Winter overheating and summer air conditioning cause dehydration that contributes to itching and dryness, compounded by the loss and poor functioning of your sebaceous (oil) and sweat glands.

The sun's ultraviolet B (UVB) rays, more intense in the summer, cause sunburn and skin cancer. Ultraviolet A (UVA) rays are of the same intensity year round and are also known to contribute to skin cancer. Therefore, your skin should be protected by sunscreen during all seasons, whether the day is sunny or cloudy. Apply it before coming in contact with the sun, since it needs time to absorb. The sunscreen should be at least an SPF of 15 and protect against both UVA and UVB. Apply moisturizer liberally, and use mild cleansers and body washes instead of soap, since the later can dry skin. No matter what your age, drink plenty of water to hydrate from the inside. Exercise promotes good circulation that helps nourish your skin. A skin-healthy diet is important as well. Some dermatologists recommend antioxidant-rich fruits and vegetables high in vitamins A and C and "good" fats such as omega-3 fatty acids found in fish that will increase the oil in your skin. As with wrinkle protection, stop smoking, and avoid fragranced laundry soaps, fabric softeners, and dryer sheets that can further damage sensitive skin.

Gray Hair
The color of your hair depends upon melanin, the same pigmented substance that produces age spots. Melanin-producing cells that surround every hair follicle inject this pigment into the hair as it grows out from the scalp. Hair has two types of pigments: dark (eumelanin) and light (phaeomelanin). Initially all hair is white, but combinations of these types of melanin produce a wide range of hair colors when they are injected. Absence of melanin production produces gray hair. The first silvery strands usually pop up around age thirty for men and age thirty-five for women. As the years progress more melanin-producing cells begin to decrease their production. One current theory regarding why this happens is that a "melanogentic clock" slows down or stops melanocyte activity and thus decreases the pigment that our hair receives. This "clock" may be determined by genes that regulate the exhaustion of the pigmentary production of each individual hair follicle. Another theory states that hydrogen peroxide, which is produced

naturally in the human body, interferes with melanin. Your body also produces the enzyme catalase, which breaks down hydrogen peroxide into water and oxygen, or at least it does for a while. As you age, catalase production tails off, leaving nothing to transform the hydrogen peroxide into chemicals that the body can release. Accordingly, the hydrogen peroxide that builds up bleaches the melanin and we go gray.

Other influences on hair color are divided into intrinsic factors: genetic defects, hormones, body distribution, and age; and extrinsic factors: climate, pollutants, toxins, chemical exposure, and possibly stress. Some researches suggest that stress results in an increase in local or general inflammation that produces free radicals; the radicals attack the melanin-producing cells and decrease their production. Scientists are beginning to gather clues that stress can hasten the graying process, but thus far they have found no good scientific evidence demonstrating a cause-and-effect relationship.

Graying hair seems to be an unavoidable effect of ageing, but there are some things you can do to avoid its onset. These factors include eating a well balanced diet, avoiding exposure to the sun, and avoiding environmental toxins, pollutants, and chemicals such as chlorine.

Many people find that having gray hair is unsatisfactory for their lifestyle or, like balding, a visible remainder to themselves and others that they're no longer as young as they were or wish to appear. If that applies to you, consult a beautician who can offer several artificial remedies to permanently or semi-permanently change your hair color to a more preferable shade.

Balding

Hair follicle growth occurs in cycles: a long growing phase, a short transitional phase, and a short resting phase. At the end of the resting phase, the hair falls out and a new hair starts growing in the follicle to begin the cycle again. Failure of the growing phase results in hair loss, usually unavoidable with age for both men and women. By age thirty approximately 25 percent of men begin balding; two-thirds begin by sixty years. The predominant hair thinning in men is male pattern hair loss, a receding hairline from the lateral sides of the head and from the top or crown that eventually meet to form a horseshoe-shaped ring of hair around the back of the head.

The rate and pattern of hair loss seems to be genetically determined. The hair's growth phase shortens, and the young, unpigmented hair is prevented from growing and maturing into pigmented terminal hairs. Hair slowly becomes thinner and reduced in volume, replaced by only early hair or "peach fuzz" until the hair follicle eventually becomes dormant and completely stops producing hair.

Besides genetic predisposition, hair loss can be influenced by nutrition, whether a limited food intake, a diet high in animal fats like those found in fast food, as well as high vitamin A or deficiencies in biotin, protein, zinc, and iron. Infection may be another cause. Hair loss can also be the result of drug intake for the treatment of high blood pressure, heart disease, diabetes, high cholesterol, and acne. Other drugs are testosterone or other anabolic steroids and chemotherapy to treat cancer. Trauma and autoimmune disease are additional causes.

Hair loss can threaten your psyche with feelings of loss of control, self-image, and youthful vigor for men and beauty for women. Most of us adjust to this event. For those who have difficulty, particularly when hair loss occurs early in life, a change of hairstyle may be used as a disguise or a hairpiece or hair-weaving for relief. Several medications that help reverse the process include minoxidil (Rogaine), a solution that slows hair loss, and finasteride (Propecia, Proscar), a pill that interferes with the production of a highly active form of testosterone. If you have one of the chronic diseases mentioned above, ask your physician whether your hair loss may be a side effect of medications. If none of these solutions are sufficient, hair transplants are available. The procedure is uncomfortable, but may be worth a satisfactory result.

Hearing Loss

Presbycusis is the term used for age-related hearing loss. Symptoms include hearing speech that seems mumbled or slurred, sounds that seem deeper and less clear, and conversations that are difficult to follow.

High-pitched sounds are difficult to hear, men's voices are easier to hear than women's, background noise interferes with hearing, and sometimes tinnitus or ringing in the ears occurs. Between the ages of sixty-five and seventy-five, 30 to 35 percent of people have either partial hearing loss, inability to hear certain frequencies, or hearing loss in one ear. After age seventy-five, this number increases to 50 percent, and at age eighty-five, 30 percent have deafness in at least one ear. Hearing declines with age more rapidly in men than in women. Sometimes the loss is so gradual that many people are unaware of it.

Heredity plays a role, and loss process can be accelerated by the cumulative effect of loud noise such as construction work, traffic, heavy machinery, and loud music. Some health conditions like high blood pressure, diabetes, heart disease, and viral or bacterial infections can affect blood flow to the ear. It also may be caused by trauma. Medications can cause diminished hearing, including aspirin and antibiotics.

Throughout your life you should always protect yourself from exposure to loud noises. Use earplugs when near power tools, lawn-

mowers, firearms, leaf blowers, and snowmobiles, and while attending rock concerts. Keep the volume of your headphones at a moderate level.

If hearing loss is suspected, consult an ear, nose, and throat doctor, or see an audiologist—an ear specialist who can test your hearing at different frequencies. If indicated, a hearing aid might be recommended. Another type of device to aid hearing is a cochlear implant. Used for individuals with severe hearing loss, these devices are implanted by an otolaryngologist in the inner ear. A physician must approve the use of any hearing device, unless you sign a waiver to voluntarily bypass this requirement.

You can work with your friends and family to cope with hearing loss. Inform all those around you of your difficulty, and ask them to speak to you while facing in your direction. Ask them to speak louder but not to shout, and to enunciate clearly but not necessarily more slowly.

Hearing loss can result in withdrawal from day-to-day activity and a feeling of isolation, but with proper treatment and the cooperation of others, your confidence can be regained.

Decreased Vision

Several changes in eye structure of your eyes occur with age. Your pupils become smaller, you produce fewer tears, peripheral vision decreases, color differentiation is more difficult, and the vitreous fluid material that fills your eye shrinks and may become detached.

The muscles that control your pupil size and its reaction to light weaken, so the eye is less responsive to ambient light. People in their sixties need three times more light for comfortable reading than those in their twenties. Older eyes become more sensitive when moving from a dark environment such as a movie theater into the sunlight (glasses with antireflective coating and photochromic lenses are helpful here). Other age-related problems include a decrease in your field of vision and in peripheral vision. Both may limit your ability to interact with others as well as increasing the risk of accidents, particularly when driving.

The most common problem is presbyopia (the prefix "presby" means "elder"), or difficulty focusing on things that are nearby. Its cause is most likely loss of elasticity of the eye's lens. A contributing factor can be a decreased strength of the muscles attached to the lens that control focal length. At first, accommodation can be managed by holding documents at a further distance until, as presbyopia becomes more pronounced, we half-jokingly complain that our arms have become "too short." Eventually, corrective glasses (readers) are needed. As we age, presbyopia worsens and several changes in your glasses may be required.

The amount of tears we produce decreases as we grow older, most pronounced in postmenopausal women. A condition called "dry eye" may result in a stinging, burning sensation, a gritty feeling, or redness. Someone with dry eye typically has more difficulty reading or working on a computer. Sunglasses that fit closely to the face will help decrease tear evaporation, while a humidifier will add moisture to the air. Artificial tears, gels, gel inserts, and ointments available over the counter offer temporary relief and provide an important replacement of naturally produced tears. Avoid artificial tears with preservatives if you need to apply them more than four times a day or preparations with chemicals that cause blood vessels to constrict. If dry eyes persist after trying these techniques, see an eye specialist to determine whether disease is the underlying cause.

The vitreous, a gel-like fluid inside our eyeball, becomes more liquid with age, causing it to pull away from the retina and causes spots, floaters, and sometime flashes of light. While this development can be harmless, the symptoms may foretell the more serious condition of retinal detachment; consulting an ophthalmologist is essential since the condition may result in blindness.

Although not inevitable, cataracts of the lens are common enough, and that they are the most common cause of blindness is reason to become aware of them. Fifty percent of Americans over sixty-five have some degree of cataract formation; it is estimated that by the year 2020, over 30 million Americans will suffer from this disorder. Opacity of the lens occurs after deposition of brown pigment that leads to disruption of the normal architecture of lens fibers and reduced transmission of light. Surgical removal of the cataract is relatively safe, and replacement of the lens with a simple or multifocal lens implant that eliminates the need to wear glasses can completely restore your vision.

Eye disorders become frequent as we age, so an annual exam is advisable to make sure that you are not developing one of the more serious forms of eye disease, including cataracts, glaucoma (increased pressure), and macular degeneration.

Dental Problems

Although tooth decay is more frequent during childhood and adolescence, it can occur later in life if you're negligent about dental hygiene. If you don't take care of your mouth, bacteria break down the enamel that covers and protects your teeth. A sticky colorless film called plaque forms on your teeth, and decay and cavities follow. The antidote is to brush your teeth, preferably after every meal with a toothpaste containing fluoride. Dental floss that scrapes away debris between teeth is also of great importance.

Tartar is formed when plaque that remains on your teeth hardens and leads to a gum disease called gingivitis, or inflammation of the gums. That condition in turn pulls away the gum tissue from the teeth and creates pockets that allow deep infection. Bacteria can then ruin the bone and tissue that support your teeth, leading to tooth loss. Regular cleaning by a dental hygienist is therefore essential.

Skeletal System

Bones become weak and joints become frayed over time, which may prevent you from enjoying activities in your retirement. You also become more likely to incur falls and fractures. Bone loss begins in our middle years when it starts outpacing bone formation. Bone condition at a level that is markedly below normal is called osteoporosis. Factors in addition to age include gender (females more than males), heritage (especially Northern European), small bones and a lean body, calcium and vitamin D deficiencies, and tobacco and alcohol use. Anyone with these risk factors should have a bone density examination.

Osteoporosis can lead to complicated bone fractures most often in the hip, leg, arm, hand, or ankle. The real danger is not the fracture itself but the complications it causes. A significant number of patients with hip fractures are unable to walk again, while 20 percent die from associated complications. Bones that do not break may become crushed and therefore unable to support the body's weight. Spinal vertebrae will crush nerves as they exit the spinal cord and cause severe pain. Posture may be affected too. Management of this problem includes a program of weight-bearing exercise, adequate intake of calcium and vitamin D, and medication that promotes bone growth. Postmenopausal women may consider estrogen replacement therapy, although this is not without risk. All decisions should be made in consultation with your doctor.

The most common midlife cause of osteoarthritis is the fraying and erosion of cartilage, which, in the worst cases, leaves bone rubbing against bone. This leading cause of disability affects 10 percent of the population over sixty years of age. You might initially choose analgesics taken by mouth, applied locally, or injected into the joints. Nonpharmacologic therapies include exercise, physical therapy, weight loss, bracing, and orthotic devices that change the amount of pressure on joints. Depression and anxiety may result from having to live with chronic pain, and these issues should be dealt with as well.

Surgery becomes an alternative if these methods do not relieve the pain and disability. Arthrodesis is a procedure that fuses two bones to eliminate the painful joint. Arthroscopy, a minimally invasive procedure, may be the choice if cartilage fragments must be removed. Joint replacement is done when no other treatments have worked. New joint surfaces are created: hip, knee, and shoulder joints are the most frequently ones replaced, but elbows and ankles can also be treated in this fashion.

Cardiovascular System

Of all retirement-age risk factors, cardiovascular disease (hypertension, coronary artery disease, heart attack, and stroke) is the most significant. By the age of sixty-five, heart disease and stroke account for 40 percent of all deaths, rising to 60 percent by age eighty-five. They are also a major cause of disability that affects quality of your life.

Changes in the structure of the heart and its function are the chief culprits. The amount of vigorous exercise you can perform decreases with age, with about half of this decline due to changes in the aging heart. The ability to perform vigorous exercise decreases by almost 50 percent from age twenty until eighty years of age. The older heart does not respond as well to signals from the brain to increase rate, while the force of contraction can increase only about 65 percent when at rest. Consequently, older people have a decrease in cardiac output. For example, a twenty-year-old can increase the amount of blood pumped per minute three and a half to fourfold with vigorous exercise, while someone at age eighty can only double the amount.

Because of changes in the stiffness and thickness of the walls of the heart chambers, there is an increase in normal blood pressure that is transmitted backwards to pulmonary veins draining the lungs. Blood cannot flow as freely, and consequently the lungs deliver less oxygen to the blood cells, and less carbon dioxide is removed in the lungs. You then breathe faster and harder and experience shortness of breath. The amount of exercise you can do before you experience this symptom depends on the heart muscular wall thickness. Tolerance to exertion can be built up by regular aerobic exercise. Fluid in the lungs can also cause shortness of breath. If you experience shortness of breath at rest or during minimal exertion, consultation with your physician is highly advisable.

High Blood Pressure (Hypertension)

Blood pressure is the measure of blood vessel activity caused by cardiac contraction that propels blood around your body. It is measured both after the heart contracts to propel blood, called systolic blood pressure (the first number) and, while the heart is relaxed and filling with blood, diastolic blood pressure (the second number). During adolescence and early adulthood, a normal reading is 120/80. Prehypertension is between normal values and 140/90. Hypertension exists above 140/90. Stiffness in artery walls occurs as you age, so most physicians consider a blood pressure of 140/90 in people over age fifty-five to be normal. These values, however, may be revised, since recently a select committee of cardiologists has agreed, after reviewing good scientific evidence, that a blood pressure of 150/90 or less is normal.

High blood pressure is a common finding with age; a study found that one-third of American adults have hypertension. Unfortunately, you may not be aware that you have hypertension since it frequently is appears without symptoms. That's the reason why your pressure should be checked at least once or twice a year, whether at your doctor's office or on a machine (frequently found at a pharmacy) where you can take it yourself.

Hypertension can lead to heart attacks, strokes, and kidney failure. Conditions besides advancing age that increase such risk include a family history of high blood pressure, being overweight, smoking, overindulging in alcohol, a sedentary lifestyle, and lack of sleep. Lifestyle changes to lower blood pressure include a diet with less salt, fewer calories from carbohydrates and fat and more from fruits and vegetables, weight loss if needed, no smoking, less alcohol, more exercise, and improved sleep habits. If your blood pressure does not return to the normal range after these changes, your doctor will prescribe one or more medications.

Swelling of Ankles and Feet
Although this symptom can come from blood clots in the arteries or veins, infection, liver and kidney disease, it is more commonly due to medications such as calcium channel blockers used to treat hypertension or diabetes, steroids, hormones such as estrogen used to treat menopausal symptoms, and antidepressants, as well as varicose veins.

A greater concern is that leg swelling may be due to heart disease. As with reduced exercise intolerance and shortness of breath, swelling of the extremities can be caused by an increase in pressure in the veins that return blood from the extremities to the heart and a decreased blood flow. Heart failure results in an inability of the heart to pump enough blood to meet the body's requirements. When the kidneys sense this reduced blood flow to organs, it sends out hormonal signals that cause the body to retain fluid. Gravity causes this fluid to pool in the lower extremities. Swelling of your legs can be a symptom of a more serious ailment and calls for a visit to your physician.

Another cause of leg pain and swelling is enlargement of the leg veins, called varicose veins. This problem is three times more common in women; over half of those who suffer from this problem have a positive family history. The cause of superficial varicose veins occurs when vein valves malfunction and prevent blood from flowing backwards; blood returns to the legs and causes swelling. Other causes are weakness of the vein wall or an increase in pressure inside the vein.

Complications of varicose veins include an ache or pressure in the legs when standing for long periods of time. Elevating the legs relieves this discomfort. Support hose, a type of compression stocking, are often effective. If the problem persists and symptoms become intolerable, or if leg ulcers develop, medical procedures to close up these veins include injecting a solution into the vein or using radio waves or a laser. Surgery can accomplish this as well. Finally, an individual may wish to have the veins removed for cosmetic reasons.

Heartburn

More than sixty million Americans experience heartburn caused by gastrointestinal reflux disease at least once a month, and fifteen million do so on a daily basis. Aging makes it happen even more frequently. The burning sensation and acrid taste are not due to an increase in the acidity of stomach acid (which actually decreases with age), but to the reflux of acid from the stomach into the lower esophagus.

Several age-related changes increase reflux. Most important is a greater relaxation of the lower esophageal sphincter (LES) located between the stomach and esophagus. Gastric contents returning upward to the esophageal lining causes the pain. Reflux increases with weight gain. The stomach takes a longer time to empty as you age, so the effect of medications such as calcium channel blockers that treat hypertension and anticholinergic agents like Ditropan that treat irritable bowel syndrome remain in the stomach longer and their effects are heightened. Another factor that causes reflux is a hiatal hernia when the relaxation of ligaments in the diaphragm allows a small portion of the stomach to enter the chest cavity and put pressure on the LES. Certain foods that cause LES relaxation include chocolate, caffeine, fatty foods, alcohol, peppermint, and cigarettes. There is also a relationship of reflux and activity: the more sedentary time you spend, the more you will experience reflux.

If heartburn is a problem, avoid the foods mentioned above and lose weight if it's above average. Avoid eating prior to two to three hours before bedtime. Proper positioning when you sleep can reduce external pressure on the LES: elevate your head on several pillows and avoid sleeping on your right side. Daily exercising also helps.

Over-the-counter medications include antacids such as Alka-Seltzer, Tums, or Rolaids, and others such as Maalox or Tagamet, Pepcid, and Zantac and Prilosec. All neutralize or reduce acid secretion. However, self-diagnosis and treatment are not without risk. Some conditions that may cause similar symptoms are a heart attack, a pre-ulcerative condition, or stomach ulcers themselves, which are important to treat more aggressively since they can lead to stomach or esophageal cancer. If heartburn persists and occurs with greater frequency, consult a physician.

Constipation

Constipation is not a disease; it is a symptom that occurs throughout life and more commonly in our later years and more commonly among women. The rate at which food passes through your system slows with age, particularly in the large colon. Storage time in that location increases, which allows a longer time for water to be reabsorbed from your feces, which makes your stool increase in size and hardness. You should be aware of this problem if you have fewer than three bowel movements in a week and difficulty in the movement, produce hard and lumpy stools, and feel that you're unable to fully empty your bowels.

Risk for constipation increases with eating high-fat meats, dairy products, sugary desserts and sweets, and soft, prepared foods (more common among denture wearers), as well as inadequate water or fiber intake. Lack of exercise is another cause, especially after bed rest during an illness or after surgery. Surprisingly, overusing laxatives or taking too many enemas, which initially help treat this condition, can make it worse; your body becomes used to these therapies and "forgets" how to function normally. Medical conditions such as stroke, intestinal blockage, or diabetes may affect muscles and nerves used for a normal bowel movement and increase constipation. Constipation is also a side effect of medications such as antacids containing calcium and aluminum and iron supplements. Others used to treat a variety of conditions such as pain (particularly opiates), allergies, high blood pressure, and Parkinson's disease will make constipation worse.

Your first efforts to treat constipation are to reverse what may be its cause. First, get enough fiber from a diet rich in bran, whole grain cereals and bread, cooked or raw fruit, or dried foods such as figs, prunes, and apricots. Add some bran to your morning cereal or psyllium seed to your diet. Drink plenty of fluid during the day. Stool softener pills and mineral oil (a teaspoonful taken in the morning) may facilitate bowel movement within one or two days. If you use mineral oil, be very careful to avoid getting any of it into your lungs since it can cause a severe chemical pneumonia. Exercise regularly and stay active. Never hold back a bowel movement for a long time, which will decrease your stool's water content. Finally, if these changes don't completely resolve your problem, consult with your doctor.

Urination Irregularities

Changes in bladder function with age lead to decreased contraction pressure and delays in signals to empty the bladder on the first contraction. Lying supine at night increases blood flow to your kidney, allowing increased kidney filtration and urine formation which is stored in your bladder. When the urge to urinate occurs at night (nocturia), your bladder contacts and the junction between your bladder and urethra (the tube that carries urine way from the bladder) relaxes so that your bladder can empty. Swelling of the prostate gland which surrounds the urethra is the main cause of frequent (more than once) nighttime urination for older men. If the urethra is blocked by an enlarged male prostate gland, most often due to benign prostatic hypertrophy (BPH), incomplete bladder emptying may occur. Although in these circumstances there is a feeling that complete emptying has occurred, the bladder remains full of urine, and a need to go happens a little while later. Other BPH symptoms include feeling that you've not completely emptied your bladder, needing to urinate within two hours, needing to find a urinal immediately, stopping and starting urination, straining, or a weak urinary stream.

Other causes of nocturia include drinking caffeinated beverages or taking diuretic medication close to bedtime. A urinary tract infection or prostate or bladder cancer, although more uncommon, may be causes as well. If evening fluid, caffeine, and medication restriction don't relieve nighttime urinary frequency, you should be evaluated for BPH by a urologist, who may recommend hormonal therapy or surgery.

Urinary incontinence becomes a common problem that seriously affects one's quality of life. Approximately 50 percent of women will eventually suffer from this problem. Several predisposing factors are being Caucasian, obesity, childbirth, and such medical problems as diabetes and stroke. Why you might experience involuntary urine loss fall into three main categories. (1) Stress incontinence, which results from an increase in abdominal pressure while sneezing or laughing, is due to a failure of the sphincter muscle, located between the bladder and urethra, to remain closed. This happens in women mainly due to lack of strength of the pelvis muscles that support the bladder, while it is almost always due in men to complications of prostate surgery. (2) Urge incontinence, a sudden urge to empty your bladder, is due to overactivity of the detrusor muscle that normally remains relaxed to allow the bladder to fill with urine. (3) Overflow incontinence, marked by dribbling, either constantly or after urination, is also due to impaired detrusor muscle contractility caused by a disturbance of nerve impulses to the bladder or by partial obstruction of the urethra. While in men the inability to void is caused by a much-enlarged prostate, incontinence is most often due to a complication of prostate surgery. In women it is a herniation of the bladder called a cystocele. Especially in older women, symptoms can combine, for example, stress and urge incontinence. Your symptoms may suggest one cause, but a visit to your physician along with necessary testing to make a diagnosis is recommended.

The first treatment is usually Kegel exercises that strengthen pelvic floor muscles. Electrical stimulation of these muscles is an alternative. If a urinary tract infection is found, it will be treated. Surgery may be recommended to reduce the size of the prostate gland in men and to provide additional support for the pelvic muscles or to reduce a cystocele hernia in women. Your doctor, who may also prescribe drugs to improve bladder function, may discontinue medications that may cause urinary incontinence. Estrogen replacement therapy has been shown to improve female bladder function, but this therapy has risks about which you should be aware. If none of these therapies works, placing a tube in the bladder for drainage, or chronic catheterization, may help, although drawbacks including urinary tract infection may occur.

Decreased Sex Drive

Retirement may give you and your mate or partner more time to spend together, including time for intimate activities. However, with age come many hormonal changes and other medical problems that can cause your interest and performance in sexual activity to decrease. Most influential among these factors is a decrease in hormonal production of estrogen in women and testosterone in men.

Decreased estrogen will result in narrowing and shortening of the vagina and its ability to self-lubricate. Vaginal walls become thinner and stiffer, making intercourse more difficult and sometimes painful. Many over-the-counter products can treat vaginal dryness, including water-based lubricants and moisturizers, which are used every two to three days. Your physician may suggest a trial of local estrogen therapy.

As television commercials point out, testosterone affects the quality and duration of male erections. A decrease in that hormone may be one of the contributing factors to erectile dysfunction (ED). ED is also amenable to therapy: pills and self-administered injections of medications that increase blood flow to the penis and increase its hardness. There are drawbacks to these therapies, particularly if you are taking nitroglycerine for heart disease. Other approaches are using a vacuum or penile implant.

It is important to realize that other diseases that you may be dealing with may complicate sexual desires and performance: chronic pain, arthritis, heart disease, depression, dementia, incontinence, stroke, and diabetes. Surgical procedures such as hysterectomy, mastectomy, and prostatectomy may also interfere with satisfying sex. So will certain medications, among which are certain blood pressure and ulcer drugs, antihistamines, antidepressants, tranquilizers, and appetite suppressants. Your physician may be able to suggest alternative therapies. Also remember that too much alcohol can cause ED in men and delayed orgasm in women.

You might think that hormonal replacement therapy for low estrogen in women and testosterone in men might be beneficial, but their side effects make physicians wary of recommending them. Estrogen and testosterone replacement therapy has been associated with an increased risk of heart disease, a connection that is presently being studied. That is why hormones should never be used unless under your physician's direct supervision.

Emotions are a major influence on any intimate relationship; how you feel has a strong influence on how you perform. Your sex life in your retirement years might actually improve since you have more time to spend together, more privacy, fewer distractions, and no worries about unwanted pregnancies. However, factors that might interfere include concerns about appearance as well as any disability that either partner is experiencing. An open and candid discussion with your partner in a relaxed moment will help foster understanding and empathy. You may also wish to seek the help of a therapist who specializes in this area.

Memory Loss

Memory loss is a normal occurrence as we age. About 40 percent of people aged sixty-five or older in the United States have age-associated memory impairment. Of this group, only about 1 percent of them each year will progress to dementia.

A decline in both the ability to learn new tasks and in short-term memory is characteristic of age-related memory loss. Then, too, when a task is interrupted and a new one introduced, the elderly individual has difficulty resuming the original activity and experiences the so-called senior moment. Several reasons have been advanced as to why the ability to learn and retrieve information declines. One view, the theory of disuse, is that retired adults don't use their brain as much as they did when they were working. Another reason has to do with a decrease in the ability to concentrate, and a third is that older individuals lose confidence in their own memory. Although the underlying disturbance in brain function that causes age-related memory loss remains to be clearly identified, an abnormality of the tissue that provides interconnections between various brain regions is suspected.

Several actions that can slow down memory loss begin with remaining mentally active and organized. "To do" lists, calendars to remember appointments, and making name associations help. Eat a healthy diet that is particularly rich in vitamin B-12, avoid alcohol abuse, and reduce your stress, depression, and anxiety. An active social life, where support is readily available, may also be of benefit. Since memory is stronger for auditory rather than visual stimulation, playing a musical instrument can help. Exercise is important since it increases blood flow to the brain. If you are taking medication for one or more chronic diseases, ask your physician to determine if medications you are taking might affect your memory. Your doctor can also check your thyroid function and look for other, more serious causes of memory loss.

If your memory seems to be getting worse and you have trouble driving or shopping, talking with a friend or finding your destination, or if your friends or family notice that you become confused or have trouble taking care of yourself, you may have a more serious form of memory loss. These include mild cognitive impairment (MCI) or a form of dementia such as Alzheimer's disease. Each form of serious memory loss has a particular set of symptoms, but they have the common consequence of markedly disturbing your day-to-day activities and can even result in loss of life.

With mild cognitive impairment (MCI), you may lose things often, forget appointments, and have more serious difficulty coming up with words; however, you can still do your normal activities and take care of yourself. Following the recommendations listed above will help, but frequents visits to your physician are very important. Your doctor may wish to give you language, memory, and thinking tests to rule out medical problems and to monitor your progress since MCI can progress to Alzheimer's disease.

Alzheimer's disease, the most common form of serious memory loss or dementia, is caused by the death of large numbers of brain cells (experts predict by the year 2050, one in eighty-five people worldwide will be affected). Alzheimer's begins slowly, manifested by the same symptoms seen with MCI, but can become life-threatening when sufferers forget how to take care of themselves, including dressing, bathing, and eating. In its most severe form, individuals must be admitted to a special nursing home or require around-the-clock supervision from an attendant in order to survive. Often even that is not enough. While several medications have been approved to slow the progress, none can reverse the memory loss that has already occurred.

Help, I've Fallen and I Can't Get Up . . . Falls

Falls are not uncommon, and every year over one-third of adults over age sixty-five experience one. The most common bones that break after a fall are the hip, arm, hand, ankle, and spine. Such an accident can lead to surgery, disability, and often prolonged bed rest.

Many factors cause falls, most commonly a combination of more than one: age-related changes in vision, muscle strength, flexibility, and endurance. Walking may prove more difficult because of poor balance, arthritis, and complications of the nervous system. Loss of reflexes may cause you to react slowly when you lose your balance.

Medications, particularly those used to control blood pressure, can result in dizziness from lowered blood pressure when you stand up. A similar blood pressure drop can also be related to dehydration, diabetes, kidney disease, infection, and neurologic disorders. There appears to be a direct relationship between the number of medications you take and a risk of falling. If you take many drugs, review your medication list with your physician, who may be able to identify one or more or interactions as the culprit.

Falling may be the result of the environment in which you live. Wearing loose-fitting shoes or those with smooth leather soles or long laces are accidents waiting to happen. Staircases are a particular area of concern if poorly lit or lack a banister. Slipping in bathtubs and showers is common, and a reason to install handrails. Articles left on the floor, particularly by children or pets, are another significant hazard.

If you do fall and become confused, wait for your mind to clear or call for help to assist you before trying to get up and walk around.

Insomnia

As you get older, your requirement for sleep returns to what it was in childhood, about seven to nine hours per night. Unfortunately, many older adults often get less sleep than they require because of the longer time that it takes to fall asleep. Also, older people often sleep less deeply and wake up more often throughout the night, which may be why they may nap more often during daytime. Nighttime sleep schedules may change with age too. Many older adults tend to grow sleepier earlier in the evening and awaken earlier in the morning.

Poor nighttime sleep can have a significant effect on your quality of life: a depressed mood, memory and attention problems, more nighttime falls, excessive daytime sleepiness, and the need for sleep-aid medications. Having difficulty with sleep is not considered to be a normal part of aging, even though it should be because half of the population over the age sixty has the problem.

Insomnia, the term used to identify difficulty with normal sleep, describes difficulty falling asleep within the normal thirty to forty-five minutes, waking up frequently during the night, and waking early and being unable to get back to sleep. Many conditions that occur more frequently with age can be an underlying cause. Since you are now retired, you may not be as active as when you were working. Not getting enough exercise will affect your sleep–wake cycle. Daytime naps and avoiding sunlight outdoors will affect circadian rhythms. Excessive coffee or alcohol can also cause sleep problems.

Short-term insomnia lasting less than a month may result from disturbing circumstances such as losing a partner, moving, losing your job, or experiencing financial difficulties. If sleep difficulties persist after these problems are resolved or improved, other factors should be considered. Male enlargement of the prostate causes a need to get up at night to urinate. Women may have problems with incontinence. Pain or other discomfort from arthritis, heartburn, menopause, or cancer disturb sleep, as do heart failure, hypertension, asthma, Parkinson's, restless leg syndrome, dementia, and depression.

Certain lifestyle changes may help overcome insomnia. Increase the amount of outdoor exercise, especially in an environment with adequate sun. Use your bedroom only for sex and sleep, not for watching TV or using your computer or telephone. Make your bedroom sleep-friendly with adequate darkness, good ventilation, and little sound. Go to bed and wake up at the same time every day. Some people find that a period of relaxation is helpful before going to sleep: read a book, listen to music, or take a warm bath. Stop work-related activity. Avoid alcohol and caffeine before bedtime. Limit daytime napping to no more than thirty minutes. Once in bed, if you can't sleep, get up and engage in a relaxing activity like reading or listening to soothing music on the radio. When you become sleepy, return to bed. Beware of over-the-counter medications recommended for sleep since they can cause profound fatigue during the day.

Sleep apnea, a problem said to affect one in twenty, is a condition caused by a blockage of air getting to your lungs that results in a pause in breathing. That pause decreases blood oxygen and increases blood carbon dioxide. The most common cause is deep relaxation of the muscles in the throat: the sufferer snores or stops breathing for a short period and then takes deep, gasping breaths. Besides disrupting sleep and causing daytime drowsiness, sleep apnea puts one at risk for heart disease, headaches, memory loss, and depression. If you've been told that you show such symptoms, your physician can perform tests to make the diagnosis and provide you with a device to clear the obstruction in your airways, for example, a continuous positive airway pressure (CPAP), which will assist breathing and alleviate your symptoms.

Depression and Anxiety

The rate of anxiety and severe depression increases in those of postretirement age. Several studies have shown that severe depression is evident in about 20 percent of people age eighty-five and older, compared with 15 percent among people age eighty-four or younger. Untreated depression is a serious problem. Individuals who are depressed abuse alcohol, nicotine, and prohibited substances to a greater extent, all of which are contributory factors in the cause and recovery from disease. In and of itself, depression can make it difficult to overcome serious illnesses.

Recent studies of patients with stroke and heart attacks examined the effect that major depression had on these two diseases. Depressed patients have greater difficulty making such health care decisions as seeking medical help for troubling symptoms, following instructions about when and how often to take prescribed medications, and taking care of themselves. For all of these reasons, it was found that patients with major depression have a higher risk of death in the first few months after a heart attack.

Individuals who are depressed also have difficulty engaging in activities that will promote and maintain health during retirement years. These include exercising regularly, eating a healthy diet, and engaging in meaningful activities and relationships. If you or anyone you know exhibits any of these symptoms, do all you can as soon as you can to see that the sufferer receives professional help.

Can We Beat the Aging Clock? . . . Delaying the Process of Aging

For centuries "snake oil" salesmen and other charlatans have touted any number of "fountain of youth" nostrums guaranteed to slow the aging process. Most have proven without benefit; however, in the last few decades, research has identified several that hold promise. These agents include antioxidants, calorie restriction, intermittent fasting, testosterone, estrogen, and growth hormones. Although some can temporarily improve various bodily functions lost during the normal aging process, all have deleterious effects, and as yet none has proven to prolong life. Currently, until further ongoing research proves otherwise, the medical and scientific community does not recommend their use unless they are administered in a carefully controlled research study or are closely monitored by their physician.

What if anything does work? In the last decades, irrefutable evidence shows that a change in lifestyle can add years to your life, particularly through changes in diet, exercise, avoiding tobacco and excessive alcohol, and becoming aware of and then doing something about potentially dangerous symptoms.

In the opening paragraph to this chapter, I mentioned that frequent monitoring by your health care provider is one of the essential things to preserve your health in retirement. Besides routine screening, examination, prescription refills, and administration of vaccines, your provider can assist you in developing tailored dietary and exercise plans.

Unless you have new signs or symptoms requiring immediate consultation, an annual visit to your with a health care specialist should be sufficient. Thanks to the Affordable Care Act, you will have no deductibles or copayments for preventive care, and you will be entitled to one free annual wellness checkup.

Before your appointment, make a list of all the issues that concern you. Include a record of all the medications you take, your diet, and your exercise program. If you have high blood pressure, use a home blood pressure monitor and bring it along to your doctor appointment along with your record of readings.

Be honest with your doctor and yourself in your answers to questions about your physical and mental health, use of such safety precautions as seat belts and your indulging in substances like tobacco and alcohol. Volunteer answers to matters the doctor might have missed. Your physical examination should include height, weight, body mass index, pulse, and blood pressure measurements and examinations of your chest, heart, abdomen, and extremities.

Men should have a prostate exam and women a complete breast and pelvic exam. Recent recommendations regarding the frequency of Pap testing indicate that after age sixty-five, most women can stop having them after three negative tests within the past ten years. Have your eyes checked every two years (including testing for glaucoma), and your hearing checked yearly. A visit to the dentist yearly or twice yearly is recommended. Routine blood tests are not always necessary. However, if your blood pressure is higher than 135/80, have your blood sugar measured to see if you are developing diabetes. If your cholesterol level has been normal, you should be rechecked every three to five years. This will be done more frequently if you have diabetes, heart disease, or kidney problems.

Other examinations include a colon cancer evaluation for everyone under the age of seventy-five. A mammogram for women should be performed every one to two years according to their risk for breast cancer, and they should also be tested for bone density to estimate their risk for osteoporosis. A baseline bone density scan is recommended for men over age seventy.

Get a flu shot every year. After age sixty you should get a shingles or herpes zoster vaccination. Anyone over age sixty-five should get a pneumococcal vaccine if you have never had one or if you received one more than five years before you turned sixty-five. A tetanus-diphtheria booster should be given every ten years.

Among the many medical specialties is gerontology, which concerns itself with diseases and conditions of the elderly. If the attention of a gerontologist would be helpful, your family doctor's referral is important to ensure that the gerontologist understands all the technical aspects of your medical problem and also to satisfy the needs of your insurance company.

I have tried in this chapter to stress the importance of maintaining your health so that you can attain the maximal amount of enjoyment in your years after retirement. To do so requires constant vigilance and active resistance to the aging process. Adverse physical and mental conditions frequently can be delayed to some degree by positive actions on your part. Of those activities that can delay the process of aging and maintain health, a healthy diet and exercise are most important, as are smoking cessation and moderate use of alcohol. The sooner you are able to establish routines to adopt these positive activities, the better you will be able to maintain your function and performance. Although you are the one who is ultimately responsible for your health, take full advantage of the many individuals and resources in your life that can help. I wish you good luck and hope that you have many happy retirement years.

Appendix A

MAKING YOUR HOME ELDER-FRIENDLY

Use the following checklists to evaluate the safety and convenience of a variety of residences: the home in which you now live, the one to which you're relocating, and the one in which senior citizen family and friends live. Walk through the dwelling with these suggestions, and then keep it handy in the event circumstances change.

Even if you're not planning on a wholesale renovation/refurnishing to comply with all the recommendations at once, replacing items as they wear out or break with more elder-friendly ones makes sense as long-term investments. Short-term investments too—thick, rubber-handled ergonomic can openers, for example—are easier to use whatever your age or dexterity level.

Outside Area
- Are walkways and driveways clear of obstructions, loose bricks, broken cement, and potholes? Repairing sidewalk pavement is customarily the municipality's job, so get on the phone or email and remind the appropriate department to get on the case.
- Are porch steps and their railing and banisters sturdy and in good repair? Are thresholds and "welcome" mats a hazard

that can be tripped or slipped over? Is there room to install a ramp in the event that you can no longer negotiate stairs?

- Is the outside lighting adequate? Shatter-proof bulbs are a sensible investment. So are light fixtures with motion sensors or photoelectric "eyes" that turn on automatically at dusk.
- Is the garage well-lit? Are stored items secured against falling or being tripped over?

Front door

- Lever handles are easier to grasp and engage than door-knobs. Does the front door (and, for that matter, all other exterior doors) have a deadbolt lock? How many extra sets of keys do you have, and does a nearby family member and/ or a trustworthy neighbor have a set?
- Does the peephole have a clean and clear glass set with a suitable height for all family members? If there's an intercom, does it function properly with signal buzzer and speaker at a volume that are audible to all residents?

Hallways and Stairways

- Are steps and stairways in good repair? Should any loose steps or treads be replaced? Replace slippery stairway carpet-ing and worn-out rubber treads.
- Are banisters and handrails secure and set at an appropriate height? Are there any "dead spot" places on the stairs that lacks a banister or a handrail?
- Is the stairway well-lit from top to bottom? Are there light switches near both the top and the bottom of stairways?

Living Quarters (Bedroom, Living Room, Study/Guest Room, and Dining Room)

- Are hallways free from obstructions, and are they wide enough and well-lit?

- Are rugs or carpets secured to floors? Do throw rugs have loose edges that risk tripping?
- Are electrical cords trip-over hazards, or are they out of the way and secured to walls?
- Beds and their mattresses should be at a height that's appropriate for the user. They're too low if your knees are higher than your hips when sitting on the bed (risers under the bed's legs elevate the height). The bed is too high when your legs do not touch the floor when sitting on the edge of the bed. If so, get a thinner mattress or box springs.
- Are lamps securely placed where they won't be accidentally knocked over, especially lamps that are on night tables? Is there a nightlight near the door to help you find the bathroom after dark?
- Are "landline" telephones and desktop computers securely placed, with cords that won't become entangled with lamps and other objects? Are telephones within easy access of beds and favorite chairs? Is there an extension in every room so that you won't have to make a mad dash—and risk losing your balance—to answer a call?
- Are there operational smoke and carbon monoxide detectors in bedrooms and guest rooms? Replace batteries every six months, typically when Daylight Savings Time begins and ends.
- Are closets well-lit? Is there ample space so that items won't tumble out when the door is opened or when you remove another item?
- Similarly, are bookshelves crammed beyond their capacity? If so, donate or otherwise dispose of books, magazines, records, CDs, and tapes that you're certain you'll never read or listen to again. Are the books you use most frequently in the most convenient spots?
- Are light switches easy to use? Consider replacing toggle switches with "rocker" panel switches, which are easier to use than older toggle switches.

Bathrooms

- Is the toilet at an appropriate height? Is there enough room to sit and stand without contorting your body and risking a fall? Would a wall handle make life easier? Is there easy access to the toilet paper dispenser?
- Are faucets easy to use? Lever handles on sinks, bathtubs, and showers require less effort than the twist variety.
- Is there a nonskid bathmat on the floor and a nonskid mat or strips on the bathtub and/or shower floor? "Grab bars" in tubs and showers are strongly recommended.
- Can you step on and off the bathroom scale without risking a fall?
- Is there enough space on counters and shelves for a hair dryer, dental rinsing devices, and other small appliances? Are wall brackets securely fastened? Are the appliances a safe distance from the sink and bathtub so they won't fall in?
- Is the medicine cabinet organized so that current drugs and other frequently used items are prominently displayed? The cabinet should contain only those items you use at the moment (if not, store the rest elsewhere).

Kitchen

- Is the floor slippery? If so, install rubber mats in work areas.
- Are a smoke and a carbon monoxide detector in good working order? Change batteries every six months to coincide with the start and end of Daylight Savings Time.
- Does the sink have easy-to-use lever handles?
- Are cabinets and drawers easy to open? Are the contents organized so that removing one won't cause others to fall out? Are your most frequently used items most easily reached?
- Is the dishwasher at an accessible height?

- Is your refrigerator/freezer well-organized, with the most frequently used items easy to reach?
- Are kitchen knives stored in a wooden block or in a separate drawer?
- Are stove, oven, microwave, and/or cooktop controls easy to read and use? Is there a cooking timer with a loud bell or buzzer? A whistling tea kettle will signal when the water has boiled.
- Is an operational fire extinguisher near the stove?
- Is the stepstool sturdy? It should have handles so that you can climb up and down without fear of falling.
- Is the counter space well-lit and easy to work on?
- Do utensils and appliances have nonslip handles, and are they ergonomically designed to be used with minimum effort?

Laundry Room

- If in the basement, are stairs safe to negotiate while you carry an armload of laundry?
- Are the washing machine and drier easily accessible and at a convenient height?
- Is there space to keep the laundry basket or hamper within easy reach of the machines?
- Are detergents and other laundry products in boxes or bottles that you can easily lift and store?
- Are there sponges with which to wipe up spills?

Basement

- Are the stairs and banisters sturdy and well-lit?
- Are the room or rooms well-lit? Is putting carpeting over concrete or linoleum floors now a good idea?
- Are storage items in secure containers that are placed where no one will trip over them?
- Are windows and doors secure against intruders?

Appendix B

SOCIAL SECURITY INFORMATION

The Social Security's website offers a wealth of online information about every aspect of the benefits can you can and cannot expect. Its interactive calculators are equally useful in addressing your individual situation.

Social Security Retirement Planner: www.ssa.gov/planners/retire/#sb=2

How The Social Security Retirement Planner Can Help You Now

This planner provides detailed information about your Social Security retirement benefits under current law. It also points out things you may want to consider as you prepare for the future. If you are looking for information, you can:

- Find your retirement age
- Estimate your life expectancy
- Estimate Your Retirement Benefits
- Use other benefit calculators to test different retirement ages or future earnings amounts
- Learn about Social Security programs

- Find out what happens if you work after you retire and are already a Medicare Beneficiary
- Learn how certain types of earnings and pensions can affect your benefits

If already near retirement age, you can:

- Discover your retirement options
- Get information about how members of your family may qualify for benefits
- Find instructions on how to apply for benefits and what supporting documents you may need to furnish
- Apply for retirement benefits

Close to age sixty-five, you can find out how to apply for just Medicare. You may need to sign up for Medicare close to your sixty-fifth birthday, even if you are still working. Some health insurance plans change automatically at age sixty-five. (If you are getting Social Security benefits when you turn sixty-five, your Medicare Hospital Benefits will start automatically.)

Disability Planning: www.ssa.gov/planners/disability/#sb=3

The disability planner will help you find out:

- How you can qualify and apply for benefits
- What happens if your application is approved
- Who can receive benefits on your earnings record
- What you need to know about receiving disability benefits
- When Medicare coverage starts for Social Security disability beneficiaries
- Disability and SSI
- Information for Advocates, Attorneys and Third Parties

In addition:

Benefits Calculators: www.ssa.gov/planners/benefitcalculators.html

Life Expectancy Calculator: www.ssa.gov/planners/lifeexpectancy.html

Benefit Amounts: www.ssa.gov/oact/cola/Benefits.html

RESOURCES

Internet

Growing Old in America:

www.nia.nih.gov/health/publication/growing-older-america-health-and-retirement study.

National Institute on Aging:

www.nih.gov/about/almanac/organization/NIA.htm.

Alzheimer's Disease Education and Referral, ADEAR, Center website:

www.nia.nih.gov/alzheimers/clinical-trials.

Alzheimer's Association:

www.alz.org.

Alzheimer's Foundation of America:

www.alzfdn.org.

Eldercare:

www.eldercare.gov.

NIH Senior Health Homepage.

nihseniorhealth.gov/http://www.cdc.gov/tobacco/data_statistics/sgr/2010/consumer_booklet/index.htm.

CDC Report on Smoking:

www.cdc.gov/tobacco/data_statistics/sgr/2010/consumer_booklet/index.htm.

Organizations

National Institute on Aging Information Center.

www.nia.nih.gov.

www.nia.nih.gov/Go4Life.

Aging of organs and systems.
Diet, exercise.
Dangers of smoking and alcohol.

Administration on Aging:

www.aoa.gov.

Resources for Health Maintenance

American Academy of Family Physicians:
www.familydoctor.org.
Exercise for seniors.
Health maintenance.

American Academy of Orthopedic Surgeons
www.aaos.org.
Exercise for Persons 60 Years and Older.
Bone health.

American College of Sports Medicine
317-637-9200
www.acsm.org
Exercise routines and injury avoidance.

American Council on Exercise
www.acefitness.org.
Exercise routines.

American Physical Therapy Association
www.apta.org.
Exercise routines.

American Podiatric Medical Association.
www.apma.org.
Foot care and walking routines.

Centers for Disease Control and Prevention
www.cdc.gov.
Preventive measures to maintain health.

Centers for Medicare & Medicaid Services
www.medicare.gov.
General health information and resources.

Department of Agriculture Food and Nutrition Information Center
www.nal.usda.gov/fnic.
www.ChooseMyPlate.gov
Dietary guidelines.

Food and Drug Administration
www.fda.gov/AboutFDA/CentersOffices/OfficeofFoods/CFSAN.
Medication Information.

National Cancer Institute
www.cancer.gov.
Physical Activity and Cancer Fact Sheet.

National Center for Complementary and Alternative Medicine
www.nccam.nih.gov.
Tai Chi for Health Purposes.

National Council on Aging
www.ncoa.org.
General questions about aging.

National Heart, Lung, and Blood Institute
www.nhlbi.nih.gov.
Health Information Center.
Portion Distortion Quiz.
Your Guide to Physical Activity and Your Heart.

National Institute on Alcohol Abuse and Alcoholism
www.niaaa.nih.gov.
Alcohol abuse.

National Institute of Arthritis and Musculoskeletal and Skin Diseases
www.niams.nih.gov.

Exercise for Your Bone Health.
Living with Arthritis.

National Institute of Diabetes and Digestive and Kidney Diseases
National Diabetes Information Clearinghouse.
www.diabetes.niddk.nih.gov.
What I Need to Know about Physical Activity and Diabetes.
Diabetes Health Sense: Resources for Living Well.

National Library of Medicine MedlinePlus
www.medlineplus.gov.
Search "Health Topics" for exercise and fitness information.

Office of Dietary Supplements
www.ods.od.nih.gov.
Dietary Supplement Fact Sheets.

Office of Disease Prevention and Health Promotion
www.odphp.osophs.dhhs.gov.
Physical Activity Guidelines for Americans.
Be Active Your Way: A Guide for Adults.

Office of the Surgeon General
prevention.council@hhs.gov.
Smoking cessation programs.

President's Council on Physical Fitness and Sports
www.fitness.gov.
Exercise and Fitness.

Weight-Control Information Network
www.win.niddk.nih.gov.
Active at Any Size.
Young at Heart: Tips for Older Adults Fit and Fabulous as You Mature.
Walking . . . A Step in the Right Direction.

BIBLIOGRAPHY

Alboher, Marci. The *Encore Career Handbook: How to Make a Living and a Difference in the Second Half of Life*. Workman Publishing, 2010.

Astor, Bart. *Roadmap for the Rest of Your Life: Smart Choices about Money, Health, Work, Lifestyle— and Pursuing Your Dreams*. Wiley, 2013.

Bamberger, Peter A., and Samuel B. Bacharach. *Retirement and the Hidden Epidemic: The Complex Link between Aging, Work Disengagement, and Substance Misuse and What to Do about It*. Oxford University Press, 2014.

Borchard, David C., and Patricia A. Donohoe. *The Joy of Retirement: Finding Happiness, Freedom, and the Life You've Always Wanted*. AMACOM, 2008.

Chimsky, Mark Evan., and Renee Rooks. *65 Things to Do When You Retire: More than 65 Notable Achievers on How to Make the Most of the Rest of Your Life*. Sellers Publishing, 2012.

Clitheroe, Paul. *Money for Life: How to Secure Your Financial Future*. Viking, 2001.

Collamer, Nancy. *Second-act Careers: 50 Ways to Profit from Your Passions during Semi-retirement*. Ten Speed, 2013.

Crowley, Steve. *Money for Life: The "Money Makeover" That Will End Your Worries and Secure Your Dreams*. Simon & Schuster, 1991.

Cullinane, Jan. *The Single Woman's Guide to Retirement*. Wiley, 2012.

Delamontagne, Robert P. *The Retiring Mind: How to Make the Psychological Transition to Retirement*. Synergy, 2010.

Donovan, Jim. *Don't Let an Old Person Move into Your Body: How to Make the Rest of Your Life, the Best of Your Life.* Austin Bay, 2010.

Eisenberg, Lee. *The Number: What Do You Need for the Rest of Your Life, and What Will It Cost?* Free Press, 2007.

Fraunfelder, Frederick T., and James H. Gilbaugh. *Retire Right: The 8 Scientifically Proven Traits You Need for a Happy, Fulfilling Retirement.* Avery, 2009.

Goldman, Connie. *Who Am I . . . Now That I'm Not Who I Was?: Conversations with Women in Mid-life and the Years Beyond.* Nodin Press, 2009.

Golson, Barry, and Thia Golson. *Retirement without Borders: How to Retire Abroad—in Mexico, France, Italy, Spain, Costa Rica, Panama, and Other Sunny Foreign Places (and the Secret to Making It Happen without Stress).* Scribner, 2008.

Greengard, Samuel. *AARP Crash Course in Finding the Work You Love: The Essential Guide to Reinventing Your Life.* Sterling, 2008.

Hannon, Kerry. *Great Jobs for Everyone 50+: Finding Work That Keeps You Happy and Healthy . . . And Pays the Bills.* Wiley, 2012.

Harrington, Judith B., and Stanley J. Steinberg. *The Everything Retirement Planning Book: A Complete Guide to Managing Your Investments, Securing Your Future, and Enjoying Life to Fullest.* Adams Media, 2007.

Hinden, Stan. *How to Retire Happy: The 12 Most Important Decisions You Must Make before You Retire.* McGraw-Hill, 2010.

Howells, John, and Teal Conroy. *Where to Retire: America's Best & Most Affordable Places.* Globe Pequot, 2011.

Jason, Julie. *The AARP® Retirement Survival Guide: How to Make Smart Financial Decisions in Good Times and Bad.* Sterling, 2009.

Larimore, Taylor. *The Boglehead's Guide to Retirement Planning.* Wiley, 2009.

Lloyd, Mary. *Super-charged Retirement: Ditch the Rocking Chair, Trash the Remote and Do What You Love.* Hankfritz, 2009.

Lubow, Joe. *Choose a College Town for Retirement: Retirement Discoveries for Every Budget.* GPP Travel, 1999.

Merriman, Paul A., and Richard Buck. *Financial Fitness Forever: 5 Steps to More Money, Less Risk, and More Peace of Mind.* McGraw-Hill, 2012.

Mitchell, William D. *Estate & Retirement Planning Answer Book 2015.* CCH Incorporated, 2014.

Pauley, Jane. *Your Life Calling: Reimagining the Rest of Your Life.* Simon & Schuster, 2014.

Piper, Mike. *Can I Retire?: How Much Money You Need to Retire and How to Manage Your Retirement Savings, Explained in 100 Pages or Less.* Simple Subjects, 2010.

Stim, Richard, and Ralph E. Warner. *Retire Happy: What You Can Do Now to Guarantee a Great Retirement.* Nolo, 2008.

Strauch, Barbara. *The Secret Life of The Grown-Up Brain.* Viking, 2010.

Warner, Ralph E. *Get a Life: You Don't Need a Million to Retire Well.* Nolo, 1996.

Woodward, Jeanette. *Finding a Job after 50: Reinvent Yourself for the 21st Century.* Career Press, 2007.

Waxman, Barbara Frey. *How to Love Your Retirement: The Guide to the "Best" of Your Life.* Hundreds of Heads, 2010.

Yeager, Jeff. *How to Retire the Cheapskate Way: The Ultimate Cheapskate's Guide to a Better, Earlier, Happier Retirement.* Three Rivers, 2013.

Zelinski, Ernie J. *How to Retire Happy, Wild, and Free: Retirement Wisdom That You Won't Get from Your Financial Advisor.* Ten Speed, 2004.

———. *The Joy of Not Working: A Book for the Retired, Unemployed, and Overworked.* Ten Speed, 2003.